6550 5   18718

abc BRITISH SHIPPING

Above:
Seaforth Maritime *Seaforth Monarch*.   *Courtesy: Seaforth*

D1080953

abc BRITISH SHIPPING

W. Paul Clegg

ST CHRISTOPHER

LONDON

IAN ALLAN LTD

First published 1988

ISBN 0 7110 1787 5

© Ian Allan Ltd 1988

Published by Ian Allan Ltd,
Shepperton, Surrey; and printed
by Ian Allan Printing Ltd at their
works at Coombelands in
Runnymede, England

Below:
Trinity House *Patricia*.
Courtesy: Trinity House

INTRODUCTION

British shipping has changed so much in postwar years that it is virtually unrecognisable. That process of change is still continuing. Alongside me, as I write, there lies a copy of Ian Allan's 1962 edition of *abc Ocean Ships*. A glance through its pages reveals information which would be almost unbelievable to anyone who has only taken a recent interest in the British shipping scene. Well known names of those times and extensive fleets have vanished. What has happened to them? Shipping companies whose names were familiar in almost every home in the land such as Blue Funnel (60 ships in 1962), British India (50 ships), Clan Line (46 ships) and Henderson Line (22 ships) have disappeared. Others which are no longer with us include Federal Steam Navigation Company, Shaw Savill and Union Castle.

Meanwhile, many other companies survive but as mere shadows of their former selves. Twenty-five years ago Bank Line was running 44 ships; now it has only five. The Ellerman Group, including the Wilson Line, had no fewer than 84 vessels engaged on world-wide liner services; numbers are now down to less than half-a-dozen plus shares in jointly owned containerships. Much the same situation applies to short-sea traders, and, in another sphere of operations entirely, to excursion steamers, whether paddle or screw propulsion.

The reasons for these changes are many. It is not proposed to go into them in detail here except to say that as far as short-sea cargo ships are concerned, the fall-off in coal shipments had a great deal of influence. Likewise, the changing habits of the holidaying public have greatly reduced the number of excursion ships.

Britain was always strong in world-wide deep-sea liner services, both direct to and from UK ports, and in 'cross-trades' (ie trading between other countries, such as between South Africa and the Indian sub-continent, and across the Pacific). Several factors have combined in the last 25 years to 'ease out' British operators, particularly since the end of World War 2. While Britain had an empire, and it is easy to forget how extensive this was, Britain provided virtually all the shipping services which were needed to 'feed' such countries with manufactured goods and return with raw materials. The start of the run down of the British merchant fleet can be attributed to the growing incidence of independence in former countries of the empire. Whether in East or West Africa, the Caribbean, the Indian sub-continent or South-East Asia, no sooner does a country become independent than, for political prestige, it wants to establish its own national airline and shipping line. With its own shipping line it invariably demands an increasing share of the available import and export cargoes, to the detriment of established traders — in this case British. Thus the UK fleets decline. Certain West African countries, even now are stipulating that government cargoes should only be handled by their own national lines, adding more problems to the survival of the British fleets.

The size of ships is also another factor to take into account. Twenty-five years ago, a cargo-only or passenger/cargo ship, fully equipped with deck cranes, was considered a big ship if it attained a deadweight of 15,000 tonnes. In fact, looking at a picture of such a ship now, one is inclined to wonder where there was space for any cargo! Modern container ships, with their capacity for up to 2,000 containers and more, can carry several times as much cargo as their predecessors.

Cost, of course, is an important part of the equation. During the 1960s when the British fleet was probably at its strongest, the UK unions demanded and received, artificially high wages. But this was not to last, because when cheap labour became more widely available on ships owned by 'third world' countries, it became increasingly tempting for UK operators to charter vessels from owners in these countries to cut costs, again to the detriment of the UK fleet.

This brings us to the vexed question of 'flagging out'. The term 'British ship' no longer necessarily only refers to a vessel registered in London, Liverpool or Glasgow. The registers of the Isle of Man and Bermuda are becoming increasingly popular because ships registered in these countries do not have to comply with complex UK labour laws in respect of

Above:
Flagship of the British Merchant Marine: The *QE2*. *Courtesy: Cunard*

employed seamen and officers. The facilities offered are cheaper wh..ch in modern parlance means they are more 'cost-effective'.

In practical terms, it should be noted that ships registered in 'Dependent Territories' can, and do, fly the British flag. For the record, these countries are those within the United Kingdom, including significantly, the Isle of Man and the Channel Islands and the following:

Anguilla
Bermuda
British Antarctic Territory
British Indian Ocean Territory
British Virgin Islands
Cayman Islands
Falkland Islands and Dependencies
Gibraltar
Hong Kong
Monserrat
Pitcairn Islands
St Helena
Turks and Caicos Islands

Many of the ships mentioned in this book are registered in the above territories, notably Bermuda, Hong Kong and the Isle of Man, but they are nonetheless British. It also follows that a ship registered in the Bahamas is not a British ship. Vessels transferred to the UK flag by, for example, Kuwait, in the current Gulf war for reasons of political expediency, are not included.

There have been other changes. The fishing fleet for example, which barely 15 years ago numbered over 500 vessels, has been reduced to a mere handful, as a result of EEC regulations. In the early 1970s it would have been possible to produce a book on British trawlers alone — now it is no longer so. The Port of Hull receives fish from upwards of 120 fishing boats, but with the exception of half a dozen, all are Icelandic. Conversely, there has been considerable growth in the offshore oil supply industry and many long-established companies (like Boston Deep Sea) as well as new ones, have been able to capitalise on this relatively recent growth area. At least there is some good news!

NOTES ON CONTENTS

When this book was first suggested, it seemed logical to divide it up into sections relating to different aspects of the shipping industry, such as cruise liners, tugs, cross-channel ferries and deep-sea container ships. In practice, however, this was found to be less than ideal because so many groups and individual companies operate a variety of craft. This would have led to duplication of company titles and other information in the various sections. All groups and companies are therefore listed throughout in simple alphabetical order with, in most cases, subsidiary companies included in the group or parent company entry. Individual company titles can easily be found in the index.

As to illustrations — there are two schools of thought on this topic — one believes that 'eye-level' views are best, while the other tends to favour the professional aerial picture, as showing the vessels' features to the best advantage. Although there are many 'eye-level' pictures reproduced here, my personal

preference is for the latter, which accounts for the extensive use of *Fotoflite* and *Skyfotos* material.

The editorial content, by and large, will be found to be self-explanatory. However, the statistical information varies from fleet to fleet. The reasons for this will be fairly obvious, but it is worth pointing out that while a tug has a bollard-pull figure, this will clearly not apply to a cruise liner, which in turn has a passenger capacity not applicable to a short-sea cargo ship. Similarly, while a deadweight figure is entirely relevant to an oil tanker, it is not significant in terms of a passenger ship or tug.

A brief explanation of each of the terms used follows:

Year
Year in which the ship was built, not necessarily the same year that it joined the company's fleet as listed.

NRT

Net Registered Tonnage. A measurement of size, not weight. It is the total cubic measurement of the earning space on a ship (ie usually the holds) expressed as 100cu ft = 1 ton.

GRT

Gross Registered Tonnage. A measurement of size. The gross tonnage is the total of virtually all the enclosed space on a ship, often with certain exceptions such as the bridge, chartroom and galley. As with NRT, 100cu ft=1 ton. GRT is always greater than NRT.

DWT

Deadweight. Usually measured in metric 'tonnes' dwt. Gives the total weight of cargo carried, ballast (if any), fresh water, fuel and persons. The dwt of a passenger liner is very low, therefore, and is virtually meaningless, while it is a critical figure for an oil tanker on the open charter market.

LOA

Length over all.

BM

Breadth.

DFT

Draft   All dimensions are expressed in metres.
The DFT shown is in almost all cases the maximum summer loaded figure. For tugs the figure is the maximum under tow.

SPD

Normal Service Speed. For tugs, the speed given is that which applies without tow (ie free running).

PAX

The figure given is usually the maximum number of passengers the ship can carry according to her certificate(s).

TEU

The number of 20ft containers (or equivalent in 40ft containers) the ship is designed to carry or is capable of carrying.

BP

Bollard-Pull. The measurement of the maximum pulling tension a tug can exert when moving away from a fixed point to which the tow rope is attached. It is measured in tonnes and can be quantified by certificate.

REG

Port Registry letters/numbers applying only to fishing vessels and certain other craft. eg 'H' indicates Hull, 'FD' Fleetwood).

The pocket histories vary in length with the least emphasis generally being given to larger companies, most of whose earlier histories have been published over the years in one form or another. Where recent and significant changes have arisen these have been included. The inclusion of these narratives here is a 'first' in any pocket book of this kind and this information has been further expanded by the inclusion of addresses, telephone and telex numbers. Also new to this kind of publication is the addition of non-cargo carrying vessels such as cable-ships and research vessels of different kinds, which will be of interest, though unfortunately Greenpeace is not included as we could not persuade them to co-operate!

An attempt has been made to incorporate as fully representative a cross-section as possible of the British merchant marine in its various forms in what is anticipated will be the first of a regular series of possible biennial publications. Details of services have been included where practicable. A great many of the ships listed are owned by banks, leasing companies, finance houses or obscure overseas one-ship companies. Details of this kind have been omitted because it is felt that they are of little value except to highly specialised interests.

Finally, a genuine effort has been made to keep as up-to-date with changing information in the book as possible but hopefully readers will appreciate that the scene is constantly changing and it would be impossible to be completely accurate given the time lag between the submission of copy and publication. In particular, the changes which are arising from the Cunard-Ellerman merger in June 1987 had still not been completed when the manuscript was finally amended. The information given in these pages is believed to have been correct at that time, but may well change by publication date.

ACKNOWLEDGEMENTS

All but a very small proportion of the information provided in this book has been supplied by the shipping companies and operators concerned, and in some cases by their public relations and marketing consultants. To all these people, many of whom are friends or acquaintances, I extend my sincere thanks for the time and trouble they have taken on my behalf. It is in my view invariably better to go to the source for first hand accurate information, rather than repeat what someone else has already printed.

For their unreserved co-operation in the matter of illustrations, I would like to thank Philip Neumann of *Fotoflite* and Charles Hamilton of *Skyfotos*. The staff of Lloyd's Register Information Section have been equally helpful; to those too, I would like to extend my thanks as I do towards Jack Gaston, John Hendy and Walter Bowie for their assistance.

Finally, to my family for their encouragement and assistance I am particularly grateful, as I am to the publishers who have been good to work with and especially patient in accepting last minute alterations with such good grace!

Paul Clegg
Ashburton
Devon

Above:
Boston Putford *Dawn Monarch*.   *Courtesy: Fotoflite*

THE ALEXANDRA TOWING CO LTD

Castle Chambers, 43 Castle Street, Liverpool L2 9TA
Tel: (051-) 227 2151   *Telex:* 627265

The company celebrated its centenary in 1987, having been founded in Liverpool in 1887. Operations in Southampton started in 1919, and in Swansea in 1924. In 1962, Britannia Steam Towing Co, based in South Wales, was acquired, which consolidated the companies' activities in the Bristol Channel, while activities on the Mersey were further strengthened by the take over of the Liverpool Screw Towing Co and its subsidiary North West Tugs — better known as 'Cock Tugs' — in 1966. Two years later, the towage business of J. H. Lamey came within the Alexandra Group. The Gibraltar operations started up in 1973. One of the group's biggest expansionist moves came in 1975, when Alexandra entered the Thames scene for the first time. At the beginning of that year, the company took control of 'London Tugs', formed in 1969 when Sun Tugs (W. H. J. Alexander & Co) joined forces with Ship Towage (London) Ltd. Subsequently, southeast UK activities have been extended to include the Haven ports (Harwich, Ipswich and Felixstowe) and Ramsgate. Haven Tugs are operated by a subsidiary, The Alexandra Towing Company (Felixstowe) Ltd, while London tugs are usually operated by The Alexandra Towing Company (London) Ltd. The company is also involved in 'offshore work and operations, owning four pontoons, two of which are over 4,000grt.

Liverpool and Barrow (*Tel:* [051-] 227 2151)

Name	Year	GRT	LOA	BM	DFT	SPD	BP
Bramley Moore (1, 5)	1984	336	33.2	9.5	4.6	13	38.5
Canada (5)	1981	258	30	9.4	4.3	12.8	32
Coburg	1967	219	32.6	8.6	4	13	22
Collingwood (5)	1981	259	30.6	9.3	4.3	12.8	32
Huskisson	1967	219	32.6	8.6	4	13	22
Indomitable (2)	1979	406.1	35	9.8	4.5	13.5	55
Nelson	1966	173	32	8.2	4	12	21
Redoubtable (1)	1975	312	40	9.9	4.5	14	70
Romsey	1964	173	32	8.2	4	12	18
Trafalgar	1966	173	32	8.2	4	12	21
Wallasey	1977	265	32	9.6	4.8	13	45
Waterloo (5)	1987	330	31	9.3	4.6	13	38.5

London and Ramsgate (*Tel:* [0474] 359361   Telex: 965558)

Name	Year	GRT	LOA	BM	DFT	SPD	BP
Avenger	1975	299	40	10.1	4.5	14	70
Burma	1967	166	31	7.8	4	12	16
Formidable	1979	406.1	35	9.8	4.5	13.5	55
Hendon	1977	266	32	9.7	4.7	12.5	45
Sun Anglia (1, 5)	1985	339	33	9.5	4.6	13	38.5
Sun Essex (1)	1977	272	32	9.6	4.8	13	35
Sun Kent	1977	272	32	9.6	4.8	13	35
Sun London	1977	265	32	9.6	4.8	13	45
Sun Swale (1, 3, 5)	1968	192	29	8.5	4.4	12.5	18
Sun Thames (1, 5)	1982	330	33	10	4.6	12	30
Sun II	1965	150	28	7.4	4	12	18
Sun XXV (1,4)	1963	231	35	8.7	4.8	13	35
Sun XXVI (1, 4)	1965	230	35	8.7	4.8	12	35
Sun XXVII (1)	1968	226	35	8.7	4	12	25
Watercock	1967	161	31	7.8	4	12	16

Haven Ports (Felixstowe) (*Tel:* [0394] 673501   Telex: 988776)

Name	Year	GRT	LOA	BM	DFT	SPD	BP
Alfred	1972	272	32	9.4	5	13.25	40
Brightwell (1, 6)	1986	256	28.5	9	4	12.5	40
Crosby	1972	272	32	9.4	5	13.25	40

Above:
Alexandra Towing Co *Sun Swale*. *Courtesy: M. J. Gaston*

Below:
Alexandra Towing Co *Indomitable*. *Courtesy: M. J. Gaston*

Above:
Alexandra Towing Co *Sun Anglia*. *Courtesy: Fotoflite*

Below:
Alexandra Towing Co *Sun XXV*. *Courtesy: Fotoflite*

Name	Year	GRT	LOA	BM	DFT	SPD	BP
Egerton	1965	172	32	8.3	4	12	18
Ganges (1)	1982	281	32	9.6	4.8	13.5	42

Southampton (*Tel:* [0703] 223677   *Telex:* 47368)

Name	Year	GRT	LOA	BM	DFT	SPD	BP
Albert	1972	272	32	9.4	5	13.25	40
Flying Kestrel	1976	224	26	9.1	5.4	11.6	36
Flying Osprey	1976	223	26	9.1	5.4	11.6	36
Sun XXIV	1962	113	27	7	3.5	12	10
Ventnor	1964	173	32	8.2	4	12	18

Swansea and Port Talbot (*Tel:* [0792] 53041   *Telex:* 48192)

Name	Year	GRT	LOA	BM	DFT	SPD	BP
Alexandra	1963	161	31	8.1	3.7	11.5	15
Fabian's Bay	1966	149	28	7.4	3.7	12	18
Herculaneum	1962	161	31	8	3.7	11.5	15
Margam	1970	278	34	9.4	4.7	13.75	40
Mumbles	1969	291	34	9.4	4.7	13.25	40
Victoria	1972	272	32	9.4	5	13.25	40

Gibraltar (*Tel:* Gib 78618   *Telex:* 2277)

Name	Year	GRT	LOA	BM	DFT	SPD	BP
Airedale	1961	158	28.6	8.4	3.3	11	17
Sun XXI	1959	183	33	7.9	5	13	19
Wellington	1961	158	31.6	8.4	4.2	11	16

Notes: (1) Fitted with fire-fighting equipment; (2) based in the Falklands; (3) based at Ramsgate; (4) licensed to carry a maximum of 65 passengers in Thames sheltered waters only; (5) Voith Schneider propulsion; (6) Aquamaster propulsion

Alexandra Marine Transportation Ltd (anchor handling tug/supply vessel)

Name	Year	GRT	LOA	BM	DFT	SPD	BP
Invincible	1983	997	64	13.8	4.7	16.5	100

ARC MARINE LTD

Burnley Wharf, Marine Parade, Southampton SO1 1JF
(*Tel:* [0703] 634 011   *Telex:* 47127)

Based on the marine sand and gravel trade, ARC Marine was formed in 1961 to operate the dredging side of the business. The company has expanded rapidly and runs a fleet of modern suction trailing aggregate dredgers. Areas of operation are mainly in the Bristol Channel, round the Isle of Wight and off the east coast of the UK between Harwich and the Humber. ARC is a member of the Gold Fields Group of companies.

Name	Year	NRT	GRT	DWT (1)	LOA	BM	DFT	SPD
Arco Arun	1987	1,042	3,476	4,500	98.3	17.4	6.3	12.5
Arco Avon	1986	1,042	3,476	4,500	98.3	17.4	6.3	12.5
Arco Humber	1972	2,804	5,487	7,000	107	20	7.4	13
Arco Scheldt	1972	837	1,583	2,100	76.5	14	5	12
Arco Severn	1973	895	1,599	2,150	78	14	5	12
Arco Swale	1970	895	1,579	2,000	80.5	14	5	12
Arco Tamar	1964	119	355	370	44	8.8	2.9	10
Arco Taw	1968	124	349	370	44.5	8.8	2.9	10
Arco Test	1971	321	594	775	60.9	9.7	3.6	11
Arco Thames	1974	1,474	2,645	3,450	95.7	15.5	5.9	13
Arco Trent	1971	321	594	775	60.9	9.7	3.6	11
Arco Tyne	1975	1,464	2,683	3,500	95.7	15.5	5.9	13

Top:
ARC Marine *Arco Severn*.   *Courtesy: Fotoflite*

Above:
Associated British Ports *Welsh Bay*.   *Courtesy: ABP*

Below:
ACT(A) *ACT 7*.   *Courtesy: ACT(A)*

Name	Year	NRT	GRT	DWT (1)	LOA	BM	DFT	SPD
Harry Brown	1962	289	634	700	51.8	9.8	4	10
New building	1988 (2)	1,042	3,476	4,500	98.3	17.4	6.3	12.5

Notes: (1) True cargo capacity (tonnes); (2) due spring 1988, name *Arco Adur*.

ASSOCIATED BRITISH PORTS (HOLDINGS) PLC

150 Holborn, London EC1N 2LR
Tel: (01-) 430 1177   *Telex:* 23913

When Britain's railway companies were nationalised with effect from the beginning of 1948, several ports and port maintenance vessels were also incorporated in the move. Since then, 19 ports have become the property of the British Transport Docks Board, whose name was changed to ABP on privatisation at the end of 1982. ABP now owns a wide variety of port maintenance craft, including launches, several small tugs, various boats, barges, and the following dredgers, all of which are based in ABP ports:

Name	Year	NRT	GRT	DWT	LOA	BM	DFT	SPD
Aberavon (1, d)	1969	757	2,113	2,540	76.2	14.9	5	11
Baglan (2, f)	1966	798	1,899	2,134	76.2	14.3	4.9	12
Cave Sand (1, a)	1968	339	1,080	1,115	62.5	12	4	10
Cherry Sand (1, a)	1968	339	1,080	1,115	62.5	12	4	10
Clee Ness (2, a)	1962	729	1,436	1,677	68	13.4	4.9	10
Fleetwood Bay (2, e)	1980	572	1,106	1,450	55	12.4	4.5	10
Goole Bight (1, a)	1958	178	325	355	36.4	8.5	3.2	9
Hebble Sand (1, a)	1964	348	869	836	47.9	11.6	4.3	9.3
Lenne Regis (1, b)	1963	348	869	836	47.9	11.6	4.3	9.3
Redcliffe Sand (1, a)	1964	612	1,424	1,783	65.3	13.4	4.8	11
Rhymney (1, c)	1960	387	710	813	50.6	10.4	4.1	9
Skitter Ness (2, a)	1964	639	1,577	1,677	75.9	13.4	4.6	11
Swansea Bay (2, d)	1966	1,394	2,941	4,100	94.5	16	5.9	12
Welsh Bay (2, d)	1971	2,000	2,837	4,996	95	16.1	5.3	12

Notes: (1) Grab dredger; (2) suction dredger. *Based at:* (a) Humber ports; (b) King's Lynn; (c) Barrow; (d) South Wales ports; (e) Fleetwood; (f) Garston.

ASSOCIATED CONTAINER TRANSPORTATION (AUSTRALIA) LTD

136 Fenchurch Street, London EC3M 6DD
Tel: (01-) 626 3233   *Telex:* 886381

Founded in 1967, ACT(A) is a consortium in which three British shipping companies came together to provide sophisticated container services between North Europe and Australia/New Zealand. By 1971 services had also been introduced between Australia, New Zealand and North America. These companies are, Blue Star, Cunard and Ellerman, each of which has shares in the ships in use. On certain trans-Pacific sailings, up to 10 passengers can be carried on board in refurbished accommodation.

Name	Year	NRT	GRT	DWT	LOA	BM	DFT	SPD	TEU
ACT 1	1969	10,428	24,699	28,306	217.2	28.9	10.8	19.5	1,414
ACT 2	1969	10,432	24,699	28,308	217.2	28.9	10.8	19.5	1,414
ACT 3 (1)	1971	10,793	24,907	27,953	217.2	28.9	10.8	18	1,294
ACT 4 (1)	1971	10,793	24,907	27,953	217.2	28.9	10.8	18	1,294
ACT 5 (1)	1972	10,793	24,907	27,953	217.2	28.9	10.8	18	1,294
ACT 6 (1)	1972	10,707	25,013	28,104	217.2	29	10.8	18	1,356
ACT 7	1977	13,245	44,150	39,712	248.6	32.3	12	19	2,158
ACT 8 (2)	1978	21,263	52,055	47,209	258.5	32.3	13	21	2,436

Notes: ACT 1-7 are owned 42.5% by Port Line, 42.5% by Blue Star and 15% by Ellerman.

ACT 1, 5 and 7 are managed by Blue Star Ship Management.

ACT 2, 3, 4, 6 and 8 are managed by Cunard Ellerman Shipping Services.

(1) Carry passengers; (2) on charter from Ellerman/Harrison.

BANK LINE LTD

Baltic Exchange Buildings, 19-21 Bury Street, London EC3A 5AU
Tel: (01-) 283 1266   *Telex:* 887392

Andrew Weir & Co Ltd managers of Bank Line Ltd originated in 1896. In 1905 Bank Line Ltd was founded to control shipping operations, which until relatively recently encompassed a wide range of services. Currently Bank Line serves South and West Pacific Islands via Panama, jointly with Columbus Line of Hamburg, and has interests in South Africa-United States cross trading. Charters may occasionally take a Bank Line ship on to other routes.

Name	Year	NRT	GRT	DWT	LOA	BM	DFT	SPD	TEU
Clydebank	1974	6,798	11,405	15,461	161.7	22.6	9.6	17	480
Forthbank	1973	6,798	11,405	15,469	161.7	22.6	9.6	17	480
Ivybank	1974	6,798	11,405	15,461	161.7	22.6	9.6	17	480
Moraybank	1973	6,798	11,405	15,461	161.7	22.6	9.6	17	480
Willowbank (1)	1980	9,428	18,236	16,511	176.1	26.5	9.3	19	768

Notes: (1) On charter to Australia New Zealand Direct Line (ANZDL) for trans-Pacific service.

All are geared combi-ships with some container capacity as indicated.

BEN LINE STEAMERS LTD. (Ben Group Services Ltd)

33 St Mary's Street, Edinburgh EH1 1TN
Tel: (031-) 557 2323   *Telex:* 72611

Ben Line's origins date from the 1820s, but the managing company's name, which still exists, Wm Thompson & Co, was formally established in 1847. Trade links were initially with the Mediterranean and North America, but the emphasis had switched to the Far East by the time the company's first steamship appeared in 1871. Ben Line Containers Ltd was formed jointly with Ellermans in 1970, an association dedicated to Far East container services. During 1974, the company expanded into the carriage of bulk liquids, and became involved in the off-shore drilling industry in partnership with ODECO of New Orleans. The group has wide interests in this sphere of operations.

Above:
ACT(A) *ACT 8*. *Courtesy: Fotoflite*

Below:
Bank Line *Ivybank*. *Courtesy: Fotoflite*

Bottom:
Ben Line Steamers *Bencleuch*. *Courtesy: Fotoflite*

Ben Line Containers Ltd. Joint venture with ownership split 80% Ben Line and 20% Ellermans. Ships engaged in UK/North Europe-Far East container services.

Name	Year	NRT	GRT	DWT	LOA	BM	DFT	SPD	TEU
Benalder	1972	20,669	55,889	49,593	289.6	32.3	13	23	3,032
Benavon	1973	20,669	55,889	49,593	289.6	32.3	13	23	3,032
City of Edinburgh	1973	20,669	55,889	48,810	289.6	32.3	13	23	3,032

The Ben Line Steamers Ltd

Name	Year	NRT	GRT	DWT	LOA	BM	DFT	SPD
Bencleuch (1)	1976	951	1,599	2,549	80.0	12.8	5.2	13
Benhope (2)	1978	26,528	39,087	72,100	22.8	32.3	14	15
Benmacdhui (1)	1976	951	1,596	2,751	80.8	12.8	5.2	13
Benvenue (1)	1974	943	1,598	2,581	80.8	12.8	5.2	13

Notes: (1) Chemical tanker; (2) bulk carrier. All world-wide trading.

BIBBY BROS & CO. (Bibby Bros & Co Management Ltd)

Norwich House, Water Street, Liverpool L2 8UW
Tel: (051-) 236 0492   *Telex:* 629241

Dating from 1807, Bibby celebrated its 175th anniversary in 1982. In the early days, sailing ships predominated, and the company soon became associated with passenger and cargo trades to and from the Indian sub-continent and Burma in particular. Times and trading patterns changed and Bibby changed with them.

The last passenger cargo ships, serving Colombo and Rangoon, were withdrawn in 1965. Subsequently, the company retired from all liner services and began to concentrate on the charter market, particularly in respect of the gas carriers, which started operations in 1968, and in bulk shipping.

Name	Year	NRT	GRT	DWT	LOA	BM	DFT	SPD
Bibby Endeavour (1)	—	—	—	—	91.6	27.4	4.8	—
Bibby Resolution (1)	—	—	—	—	97.3	25.8	4.8	—
Bibby Venture (1)	—	—	—	—	99.2	28.5	4.8	—
Devonshire (2)	1974	21,429	32,060	38,705	207	31.4	11.3	16.5
Hampshire (2)	1974	21,429	32,060	38,678	207	31.4	11.3	16.5
Lancashire (2)	1972	1,272.2	2,526.8	3,370	88.1	13.8	6.4	13
Lincolnshire (2)	1972	12,271.1	19,799.5	24,950	187.7	26.8	9.8	16.5
Staffordshire (2)	1977	32,073	45,310.7	56,188	226.3	34.2	13	16.5
Wiltshire (2)	1968	5,630.3	10,035.9	12,518	151.7	21.3	8.2	15.5
York Marine (3)	1975	45,099.9	60,814.3	112,744	260.3	4.1	15.2	14

Notes: (1) These are 'coastels' — floating accommodation units; (2) liquefied gas carriers; (3) oil tanker.

BLUE STAR SHIP MANAGEMENT LTD

Albion House, Leadenhall Street, London EC3A 1AR
Tel: (01-) 488 4567   *Telex:* 888298

Dating from 1911, Blue Star became a household name for refrigerated meat cargoes from Australia/New Zealand, and South America, along with superb accommodation for passengers. Lamport & Holt,

of Liverpool, came within the group in 1944, followed by the Booth Steamship Co Ltd in 1946. Throughout, the Blue Star Group has been a Vestey organisation (specialising in the transport of overseas

Bibby Bros & Co *Lincolnshire*. *Courtesy: Bibby/Fotoflite*

Above:
Blue Star *English Star*. *Courtesy: Fotoflite*

Below:
Blue Star/Lamport & Holt *Churchill*. *Courtesy: Fotoflite*

Bottom:
Bolton Maritime (Nosira Shipping) *Nosira Lin*. *Courtesy: Fotoflite*

meat produce). In 1975, Blue Star Ship Management Ltd was formed to takeover the management of ships owned by the three separate companies. Currently, Blue Star is involved in liner services, is part of ACT(A) (qv), and world-wide reefer tramp-ing. Booth Line maintains its traditional services between the UK and north and northeast South America, but with chartered foreign tonnage, while Lamport & Holt concentrates on services to eastern and southeastern ports of South America.

Name	Year	NRT	GRT	DWT	LOA	BM	DFT	SPD	TEU
Auckland Star (1)	1986	4,671	10,291	11,434	151	22	8.7	20	—
Australia Star	1987	8,931	17,082	16,114	168.8	25.5	9.4	19	721
Canterbury Star (1)	1986	4,671	10,291	11,434	151	22	8.7	20	—
Churchill (2)	1979	7,204	22,635	16,114	207.3	29.2	9.4	19	1,143
English Star (1)	1986	4,671	10,291	11,434	151	22	8.7	20	—
Scottish Star (1)	1985	4,671	10,291	11,434	151	22	8.7	20	—
Southland Star (3)	1967	6,503	11,393	12,310	168.3	22.3	10	20	348
Wellington Star (3)	1967	6,503	11,393	12,326	168.3	22.8	10	20	348

Notes: (1) Reefer ships; (2) Lamport & Holt service (12 pax); (3) carries 2 pax.

BOLTON MARITIME MANAGEMENT LTD

Corn Exchange Building, 52/57 Mark Lane, London EC3R 7ST
Tel: (01-) 709 0722   *Telex:* 883549

Bolton Maritime Management was created jointly by Carnival Cruise Lines' subsidiary Nosira Shipping in 1982, when the latter acquired The Bolton Steam Shipping Company, itself founded in 1884. Ownership transferred to the UK property group Mountleigh in October 1987. The company specialises in dry bulk cargoes with geared tonnage, tramping on a world-wide basis.

Managers for:

The Bolton Steam Shipping Co Ltd

Name	Year	NRT	GRT	DWT	LOA	BM	DFT	SPD
Rubens	1976	11,236	17,966	30,160	190	23	10.7	15

Nosira Shipping Ltd

Nosira Lin	1981	11,561	18,040	30,900	188	23	10.65	15
Nosira Madeleine	1982	11,561	18,039	30,900	188	23	10.65	15

Caribbean Trailer Ships Ltd

Nosira Sharon	1981	11,561	18,039	30,900	188	23	10.65	15

BRITISH DREDGING AGGREGATES LTD

Avondale House, Avondale Road, Cardiff CF1 7XB
Tel: (0222-) 388 666   *Telex:* 498449

Established in Cardiff in 1896 as a road haulage business under the name F. Bowles & Son. Dredging in the Bristol Channel for sand started in 1920 as an additional activity. In 1932 the British Dredging Co Ltd was formed. By the early sixties, various mergers had taken place and in 1962 a new public company was formed under the same name. All four ships are of the trailing suction type and operate in the Bristol Channel.

Above:
British Dredging *Peterston*. *Courtesy: Fotoflite*

Name	Year	NRT	GRT	DWT	LOA	BM	DFT	SPD
Bowcross	1967	487.4	968.3	1,786	59.8	12	4.3	9
Bowqueen	1963	619	1,238	1,577	78.3	12.1	4.6	11
Peterston	1961	295.3	747.5	748	53.6	10.2	4.3	8
Welsh Piper	1987	375	1,251	1,923	68.9	12.3	3.9	11

BP SHIPPING LTD

BP House, Third Avenue, Harlow, Essex CM19 5AQ
Tel: (0279) 447000   *Telex:* 888811

As the shipping arm of the BP Oil Company, this company was founded in 1915 to operate ships on a world-wide basis. Later, it was found expedient to separate vessels on coastal and short-sea services, so that BP Oil Ltd was set up in 1947. Most of these smaller vessels are now almost exclusively engaged on these short-sea routes. The parent company was 'privatised' in November 1987.

Name	Year	NRT	GRT	DWT	LOA	BM	DFT	SPD
BP Battler (1)	1968	750	1,545	2,228	75.9	12.5	4.7	11
BP Harrier (1)	1980	1,052	1,595	3,120	82	15	4.7	14
BP Hunter (1)	1980	1,052	1,595	3,120	82	15	4.7	14
BP Jouster (1)	1972	771	1,598	2,342	78.9	12.6	5.2	12
BP Springer (1)	1969	493	1,077	1,562	65.5	11.3	4.4	11
BP Warrior (1)	1968	762	1,529	2,257	75.9	12.5	4.7	11
British Beech	1964	7,549	12,973	21,093	171	22.5	9.4	14
British Esk	1973	9,664	15,644	25,580	171.5	25	9.6	15
British Forth	1973	9,550	15,540	25,551	171.2	25	9.6	14
British Norness	1973	108,735	132,942	269,349	338.3	53.6	20.6	15
British Ranger	1976	108,525	133,035	269,881	338.6	53.7	20.7	15
British Reliance	1975	108,525	133,035	269,757	338.6	53.7	20.7	15
British Renown	1974	108,854	133,035	270,025	338.6	53.7	20.7	15
British Resolution	1974	108,853	133,035	279,665	338.6	53.7	20.7	15
British Resource	1975	111,080	131,535	267,913	338.7	53.7	20.7	15
British Respect	1974	112,534	136,601	277,747	336	55.3	21.2	17
British Security	1969	8,783	15,095	24,277	169.6	24.8	9.5	14
British Skill	1983	41,323	66,034	117,353	261	39.6	17.3	14
British Spirit	1982	41,331	66,024	117,353	261	39.6	17.3	14
British Success	1983	41,323	66,034	117,353	261.3	39.6	17.3	14
British Tamar	1973	9,650	15,642	25,498	171.5	25	9.6	14
British Tay	1973	9,660	15,650	25,650	171.5	25	9.5	14
British Tenacity	1969	8,792	15,095	24,277	169.6	24.8	9.5	15
British Trent	1973	9,675	15,653	25,550	171.5	25	9.6	15
British Trident (2)	1974	108,853	133,035	275,333	388.6	53.7	20.7	15
British Wye	1974	9,658	15,649	25,600	171.5	25	9.6	14
Gas Enterprise (3)	1977	28,724	43,734	53,500	231.1	34.9	13.5	20

Notes: (1) Operated by **BP Oil Ltd**, BP House, Victoria Street, London SW1E 5NJ. *Tel:* (01-) 821 2450   *Telex:* 881115; (2) on charter from P&O; (3) LPG carrier.
BP also operates a number of tankers under the Australian and Bahamaian flags.

Centre left:
BP Oil *BP Hunter*.   *Courtesy: Fotoflite*

Bottom left:
BP Shipping *British Reliance*.   *Courtesy: Fotoflite*

BRITISH TELECOM INTERNATIONAL

Central Marine Depot, Berth 203, Western Docks, Southampton SO1 0HH
Tel: (0703) 775577

In 1858 the first trans-Atlantic cable was laid, a scheme promoted by the British and US Governments, each of which supplied a warship to cover half the distance, the lines being joined in the centre. By then, cables were already in use across the Channel and in the Mediterranean. It was in 1866 that the *Great Eastern* laid a trans-Atlantic cable for the first time in one continuous length.

In 1870, all private UK inland telegraph companies were brought under the control of the GPO by Act of Parliament, and from then on the operation of such cable and cable-repair ships was maintained by the GPO until being transferred to British Telecom on its separation from the GPO in 1983. British Telecom (and BTI) were privatised in 1986.

Name	Year	NRT	GRT	DWT	LOA	BM	DFT	SPD
C. S. Alert (1)	1961	2,351	6,083	—	127.1	16.6	7.1	14
C. S. Iris (2)	1976	1,494	3,874	2,151	97.3	15	4.8	15
C. S. Monarch (2)	1975	1,494	3,874	2,151	97.3	15	4.8	15

Notes: (1) Cable-layer; (2) cable-layer and repair ship.

BROMLEY SHIPPING PLC

Imperial House, 21-25 North Street, Bromley, Kent BR1 1SJ
Tel: (01-) 290 0105   *Telex:* 896024

Founded in 1987, Bromley Shipping took over three former Irish flag vessels to take advantage of the UK government's Business Expansion Scheme, which allows investors to put up cash for a new

venture which can then be offset against taxes. The ships trade on near-Continental routes, including the Rhine and the Seine, with bulk dry cargoes including grain, fertilisers and coal.

Name	Year	NRT	GRT	DWT	LOA	BM	DFT	SPD
Union Jupiter	1977	398	699	1,010	60	9.5	3.3	10
Union Pearl	1977	398	699	1,010	60	9.5	3.3	10
Union Saturn	1977	398	699	1,010	60	9.5	3.3	10

BURIES MARKES (SHIP MANAGEMENT) LTD

65 Kingsway, Holborn, London WC2B 6TD
Tel: (01-) 242 4424   *Telex:* 884101

Buries Markes Ltd was founded in 1930, and has specialised throughout in bulk cargoes, on a tramp, world-wide basis.

Later the management company was formed to manage ships owned by both Buries Markes and others.

Name	Year	NRT	GRT	DWT	LOA	BM	DFT	SPD
Ashfield (1)	1975	1,978	4,182	6,442	111.5	16.7	7.1	16.5
Borrenmill (2)	1974	12,385	24,787	39,001	178	29.1	11.6	17
Brierfield (2)	1981	11,653	26,942	38,695	183.1	29.5	11.8	13
Chelsfield (2)	1984	12,649	27,818	41,646	187.5	29	12.1	13
Harefield (2)	1985	12,649	27,818	41,646	187.5	29.5	12.1	13
La Bahia (1)	1972	1,035	1,599	3,439	100.7	14.6	5.9	16
La Chacra (3)	1982	30,152	41,881	77,300	230	32.3	14.9	14

Above:
British Telecom *CS Iris*. *Courtesy: Fotoflite*

Below:
Bromley Shipping *Union Pearl*. *Courtesy: Fotoflite*

Bottom:
Buries Markes *La Pampa*. *Courtesy: Fotoflite*

Top:
Buries Markes *Silvermerlin*. *Courtesy: Fotoflite*

Above:
Buries Markes *Westfield*. *Courtesy: Fotoflite*

Below:
Burmah Oil *Burmah Endeavour*. *Courtesy: Burmah Oil*

Name	Year	NRT	GRT	DWT	LOA	BM	DFT	SPD
La Colina (1)	1976	1,144	1,599	3,455	96	14.1	5.5	13.8
La Falda (1)	1972	1,035	1,599	3,439	100.7	14.6	5.9	16
La Hacienda (1)	1969	675	1,452	2,365	80.5	12.7	5.2	13
La Pampa (3)	1982	30,183	41,934	77,300	230	32.3	14.9	14
La Pradera (1)	1976	1,144	1,599	3,455	96	14.1	5.5	13.8
La Quinta (1)	1969	675	1,452	2,256	80.5	12.7	5.2	13.5
Larkfield (2)	1974	12,385	24,787	39,011	182	29	11.6	14.5
Petersfield (2)	1985	12,649	27,818	41,649	187.5	29.5	11.6	13
Princefield (2)	1974	12,385	24,787	38,325	182	29	11.6	14.5
Richfield (2)	1974	12,385	24,787	39,082	182	29.1	11.6	14.5
Silverfalcon (1)	1966	661	1,301	1,940	77.3	12.7	4.8	12
Silvermerlin (1)	1968	639	1,259	1,901	77.3	12.3	4.8	12
Summerfield (2)	1974	12,385	24,787	39,008	182	29.1	11.6	14.5
Westfield (2)	1985	12,649	27,818	41,619	187.5	29.5	12.1	13

Notes: (1) Oil and/or chemical tanker; (2) geared bulk carrier with capacity for 1,584 TEUs; (3) gearless bulk carrier.

BURMAH OIL TRADING LTD

68 Mount Street, London W1Y 5HL
Tel: (01-) 499 9533   *Telex:* 8813598

Founded in 1902, Burmah Oil expanded its activities and registered a new company (as above) in London in 1908. The company specialises in the carriage of oils, both crude and refined, on a world-wide basis.

Name	Year	NRT	GRT	DWT	LOA	BM	DFT	SPD
Burmah Endeavour	1977	183,336	231,629	457,841	378.4	68	25	16
Burmah Enterprise	1978	183,336	231,629	457,927	378.4	68	25	16

CABLE & WIRELESS (MARINE) LTD

East Saxon House, 27 Duke Street, Chelmsford, Essex CM1 1HT
Tel: (0245) 260881   *Telex:* 23181

John Pender, the former founder of what is now known as Cable & Wireless was mainly responsible for laying the first permanent trans-Atlantic cable in 1866. Since then, the company has laid cables world-wide, and ships are based in Singapore, Vigo (Spain), Suva (Fiji), and the North Pacific. The parent company was 'privatised' in 1986.

Name	Year	NRT	GRT	LOA	BM	DFT	SPD
Cable Enterprise	1964	1,386	4,358	113.6	14.9	5.8	13
Cable Guardian	1984	1,839	6,133	115.6	18	6.3	10
Cable Protector (1)	1976	699	1,599	81	17	4.7	10
Cable Venture (2)	1962	3,431	9,019	151.9	18.8	8.9	12
Mercury	1962	3,333	8,962	144.4	17.9	7.6	14.5
Retriever	1962	1,469	4,218	112.8	14.5	5.8	13
New building	1988	1,839	6,133	115.6	18	6.3	10

Notes: (1) Is a multi-role support vessel; all others are cable ships; (2) is used exclusively for cable-laying, others being employed in cable maintenance and repair.

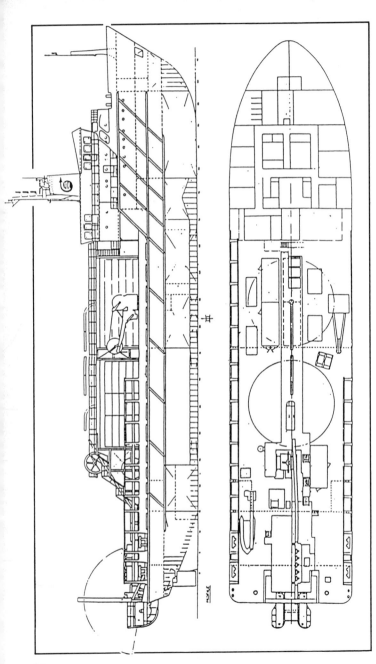

Above:
Cable Protector — deep sea cable repair ship.

Below:
Cable & Wireless Cable Guardian. *Courtesy: Cable & Wireless*

CALEDONIAN MACBRAYNE LTD

The Ferry Terminal, Gourock PA19 1QP
Tel: (0475) 33755   *Telex:* 779318

'Cal Mac' as it is known, was formed in 1972 by amalgamating, under the control of Scottish Transport Group (a state-owned body), The Caledonian Steam Packet Co Ltd and David MacBrayne Ltd. Each had, with its predecessors, roots in the very early days of steam communication in Western Scotland. Today, the company provides no fewer than seven different services on the Clyde, and nineteen in the Western Isles, serving in all 23 Scottish islands. With but two exceptions (see below) all ships carry cars and commercial vehicles on a ro-ro basis, as well as passengers.

Name	Year	NRT	GRT	LOA	BM	DFT	SPD	PAX
Bruernish	1973	34	69	22.6	6.4	1.5	8	164
Canna	1975	34	69	22.6	6.4	1.5	8	164
Claymore	1978	450	1,631	76.2	15.5	3	15	500
Coll	1974	34	69	22.6	6.4	1.5	8	154
Columba	1964	709	1,420	71.6	14	2.7	14.5	870
Eigg	1975	34	69	22.6	6.4	1.5	8	164
Glen Sannox	1957	470	1,269	78.3	14	2.4	16.5	1,100
Hebridean Isles	1985	912	3,040	84.4	16.2	3	15	500
Iona	1970	503	1,324	74.4	14	3	16	554
Isle of Arran	1984	988	3,296	84.1	16.2	3	16	800
Isle of Cumbrae	1977	90	201	37.8	10.1	1.2	10	160
Isle of Mull	1988	—	4,300	83.3	16.2	3	16	1,000
Juno	1974	305	854	69.2	13.7	2.4	14	674
Jupiter	1974	306	849	69.2	13.7	2.4	14	658
Keppel (1)	1960	131	214	33.5	8.2	1.5	9	200
Kilbrannan	1972	28	64	21	6.4	1.5	8	148
Kyleakin	1970	101	225	34.1	12.8	1.2	8	200
Lochalsh	1971	101	225	34.1	12.8	1.2	8	200
Loch Linnhe	1981	77	206	33.5	9.8	1.5	9	203
Lochmor (2)	1979	68	189	30.8	7.9	1.8	10	130
Loch Ranza	1987	77	206	35.4	9.8	1.5	9	203
Loch Riddon	1981	77	206	35.4	9.8	1.5	9	203
Loch Striven	1986	77	206	35.4	9.8	1.5	9	203
Morvern	1973	28	64	21	6.4	1.5	8	142
Pioneer	1974	356	1,071	67.4	13.4	2.4	16	356
Raasay	1976	34	69	22.6	6.4	1.5	8	164
Rhum	1973	34	69	22.6	6.4	1.5	8	164
Saturn	1978	303	851	69.2	14	2.4	14	694
Suilven	1974	851	1908	86.6	15.5	4	15.5	408
New building (573)	1989	?	?	80.2	16.2	3	16	500

Notes: (1) Usually used for cruise schedules between resorts on the Clyde (summer);
(2) small inter-island ship; vehicle (handled by crane).

CANADA MARITIME SERVICES LTD

Station Road, Horley, Surrey RH6 9HJ
Tel: (0293) 778200   *Telex:* 878448

Canada Maritime Services is the management company for ships owned by Canada Maritime Ltd of Hamilton, Bermuda. Although founded in 1984, the latter owned no ships until October 1987 when the two listed below were acquired. Prior to that, the company had chartered ships from one or the other of joint

Above:
Caledonian MacBrayne *Iona*. *Courtesy: CalMac/J. Aikman Smith*

Below:
Caledonian MacBrayne *Isle of Arran*. *Courtesy: CalMac/J. Aikman Smith*

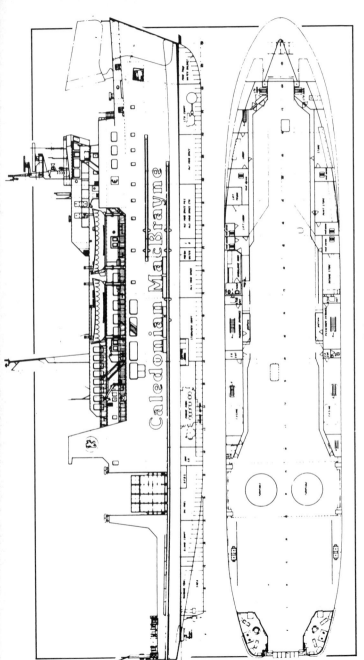

Above:
West of Scotland inter-island multi-purpose ferry
***Hebridean Isles* operated by Caledonian MacBrayne.**
Courtesy: Cochrane Shipbuilders

Below:
Caledonian MacBrayne *Lochmor.* *Courtesy: CalMac/J. Aikman Smith*

owners, Canadian Pacific (57%) and Cie. Maritime Belge (43%). The company is engaged in providing container and conventional/ro-ro services separately between the St Lawrence and Northern Europe, and container services only between the St Lawrence and the Mediterranean, on which these two operate.

Name	Year	NRT	GRT	DWT	LOA	BM	DFT	SPD	TEU
CanMar Venture	1971	7,246	15,680	16,963	167.1	25.7	9.2	18	793
San Lorenzo	1971	7,246	15,680	16,963	167.1	25.7	9.2	18	793

CANADIAN PACIFIC LTD

PO Box 6042, Station A. Montreal, Quebec, Canada H3C 3E4
London Office: Southside, 105 Victoria Street, London SW1E 6QT
Tel: (01-) 798 9898   Telex: 888373

Founded as a Canadian Railway company in 1881, CP started ship-owning on the Great Lakes three years later. Deep sea operations began in 1886, with sailing ships. Over the years the company developed its prestigious trans-oceanic passenger liner services, the last being on the Atlantic in 1971. Since then the company has placed more emphasis on its dry cargo and bulk tanker operations, though it still has an interest in trans-Atlantic container services, with gearless ships. Chartering-out and chartering-in are prominent features of CP operations today. Most dry bulk ships are geared. Many ships listed below are owned by CP subsidiary companies.

Bulk Carriers and Oil Tankers

Name	Year	NRT	GRT	DWT	LOA	BM	DFT	SPD
Carleton Progress (1)*	1978	8,753	14,088	22,174	160.9	23	7.8	15
Coulonge (2)*	1976	12,174	18,744	31,275	170.7	26	11	15.4
Edmonton (2)*	1975	12,174	18,744	31,275	170.7	26	11	15.4
Fort Assiniboine (3)	1980	11,923	19,982	31,766	169.5	27.2	11.2	14.9
Fort Calgary (1)*	1976	13,609	21,893	35,981	184	28.1	11.1	15.6
Fort Dufferin (1)*	1983	22,197	35,808	63,880	225	32.3	13.1	16.4
Fort Frontenac (1)*	1983	22,199	35,808	63,880	225	32.3	13.1	16.4
Fort Garry (3)	1975	11,293	19,982	31,674	169.5	27.2	11.2	14.9
Fort Kipp (2)*	1975	12,174	18,744	31,275	170.7	26	11	15.4
Fort MacLeod (2)*	1974	12,174	18,744	31,275	170.7	26	11	15.4
Fort Nanaimo (1)*	1975	13,623	21,894	35,982	184	28.1	11.1	15.6
Fort Nelson (1)*	1975	13,623	21,894	35,982	184	28.1	11.1	15.6
Fort Providence (1)*	1982	26,372	36,341	64,584	224.4	32.2	13	16.5
Fort Resolution (1)*	1982	24,044	64,584	36,284	224.4	32.2	13	16.5
Fort Rouge (3)	1980	11,923	19,982	31,728	169.5	27.2	11.2	14.9
Fort Steele (2)	1974	12,174	18,744	31,275	170.7	26	11	15.4
Fort Toronto (3)	1981	11,923	19,982	31,743	169.5	27.2	11.2	14.9
Fort Yale (1)*	1977	10,743	17,281	28,323	172.8	25.5	10.4	16.1
G. A. Walker (2)*	1973	12,174	18,744	31,096	170.7	26	11	15.4
Kamloops Progress (1)*	1976	10,743	17,281	28,323	172.8	25.5	10.4	16.1
R. A. Emerson (2)	1973	12,174	18,744	31,096	170.7	26	11	15.4
Victus (1)*	1977	10,743	17,281	28,323	172.8	25.5	10.4	16.1
W. A. Mather (2)*	1973	12,174	18,744	31,096	170.7	26	11	15.4

Notes: (1) Dry bulk carriers; (2) oil and products carriers; (3) chemical carriers.
   * Sold US interests Flag unknown.

Container Ships

Name	Year	NRT	GRT	DWT	LOA	BM	DFT	SPD	TEU
CanMar Ambassador	1971	13,384	30,817	29,204	231.6	30.6	10.6	21.5	1,852
Singapore Senator (1)	1979	7,947	15,504	18,674	177	27.1	10.1	19	1,061

Notes: (1) On charter to Senator Linie of West Germany.

Above:
Canadian Pacific *Fort Dufferin* (since sold). *Courtesy: Canadian Pacific*

Below:
Canadian Pacific *Fort Macleod* (since sold). *Courtesy: Canadian Pacific*

Bottom:
Canadian Pacific *CanMar Ambassador* (as *CP Ambassador*).
Courtesy: Canadian Pacific

Above:
Cenargo *Merchant Principal*. *Courtesy: Cenargo*

Below:
Cenargo *Scirocco*. *Courtesy: Cenargo*

CENARGO BROKING SERVICES LTD

12 Grosvenor Place, London SW1X 7HH
Tel: (01-) 235 9801   *Telex:* 8953256

The Cenargo group, founded in 1979, first appeared in the public eye in 1983, when it secured the contract to provide shipping services for materials and equipment to build the new Mount Pleasant airport on the Falkland Islands. Group companies own a variety of ships, most of which are dry cargo/bulk carriers, managed by Denholm Ship Management on world wide trading. The Group also incorporates Merchant Ferries, which operates a ro-ro/driver service between Heysham and Warrenpoint (Irish Sea).

Name	Year	NRT	GRT	DWT	LOA	BM	DFT	SPD
Merchant Patriot (1)	1980	8,871	16,482	21,310	164.6	26.1	10.7	17
Merchant Pilot (1)	1981	9,192	15,176.6	25,400	184.6	22.8	10.2	13
Merchant Pioneer (2)	1973	8,395.9	12,320.5	18,080	161.4	22.3	9.9	15
Merchant Prelude (1)	1980	9,337.5	15,313.3	25,400	184.6	22.8	10.2	13
Merchant Principal (2)	1978	8,752.3	14,123.8	17,944	163.1	23	9.7	15
Merchant Venture (4)	1979	1,191	2,933	3,890	119.4	17.5	5.2	18
Scirocco (3)	1974	4,697.4	8,987.4	—	130.1	22.6	5.2	19.5
Viking Trader (4)	1977	1,858.5	3,958.8	3,775.9	144.1	18.1	4.6	17

Notes: (1) Geared, self-trimming bulker; (2) geared, general cargo tween-decker; (3) (1,400 pax; 296 cars), on charter to Mediterranean owners; (4) commercial vehicle ro-ro ferry.

CENTRAL ELECTRICITY GENERATING BOARD

South-Eastern Region, Bankside House, Sumner Street, London SE1 9JU
Tel: (01-) 261 2000   *Telex:* 25815

On nationalisation in April 1948, the then British Electricity Authority acquired several colliers, 12 from the London Power Co Ltd, six from Fulham Borough Council and one from Brighton Corporation. The first ships to be built specifically for the BEA appeared two years later. Over the years many power stations on the Thames were closed down and there was no longer any need for a big fleet of small colliers. The BEA was renamed the Central Electricity Authority in 1954, which in turn became the CEGB in 1958.

Name	Year	NRT	GRT	DWT	LOA	BM	DFT	SPD
Lord Citrine	1986	6,275	14,201	22,447	154.9	24.5	8	12
Lord Hinton	1986	6,275	14,201	22,447	154.9	24.5	8	12
Sir Charles Parsons	1986	6,275	14,201	22,530	154.9	24.5	8	12

Notes: All the above are managed by Christian Salvesen (Shipping) Ltd, are gearless and engaged almost entirely in moving coal from north-eastern England and near Continental ports to Thames and Medway power stations.

H. CLARKSON & CO LTD

12 Camomile Street, London EC3A 7BP
Tel: (01-) 283 8955   *Telex:* 887811

A member of the Horace Clarkson plc Group, the company was established in 1852 as a shipbroking business, with clients worldwide. Insurance, other financial services and shipowning followed. No services are operated, ships being chartered out to others.

Top:
CEGB Sir Charles Parsons. Courtesy: YARD Ltd

Above:
H. Clarkson Santa Marta. Courtesy: Fototflite

Below:
Clyde Marine Motoring Kenilworth. Author

Name	Year	NRT	GRT	DWT	LOA	BM	DFT	SPD	TEU
Mariana (2)	1982	1,285	1,598	1,665	83	14.3	4.3	12	Nil
Sea Guardian (3)	1982	798	1,599	2,972	67.4	17.2	6.1	12.5	Nil
Santa Marta (1)	1978	3,278	5,480	6,596	119	19	6.7	17	352
Scandutch Province	1977	3,278	5,480	6,596	119	19	6.7	17	352

Notes: (1) Geared ro-ro ships; (2) LPG carrier (Clarkson share 27%); (3) off-shore service vessel. The company also owns *Earl Granville* (on charter to Sealink British Ferries — qv) and has a 50% interest in a Grimsby fishing fleet.

CLYDE MARINE MOTORING CO LTD

Princess Pier, Greenock, Renfrewshire PA16 8AW
Tel: (0475) 21281 *Telex:* 779129

Established in 1913 to provide ship/shore and mooring services to shipping on the Clyde at Greenock and Tail of the Bank anchorage, work which is still carried out. More recently the company has also become involved in local passenger services (no vehicles) and light towage on the Upper Clyde.

Passenger Vessels

Name	Year	PAX	NRT	GRT	LOA	BM	DFT	SPD
Fencer	1976	50	8	18	10.9	4	1.2	9
Hunter	1970	32	11	18	12.7	3.7	1	11
Kenilworth	1936	150	18	44	18.3	6.7	1.5	8.5
Rover	1964	120	23	48	19.8	4.9	1.2	10.5
The Second Snark	1938	120	30	45	22.9	4.9	1.2	10

Note: Two new buildings are to appear in 1988, each of 43 grt, 19.9 × 4.6m. Maximum passenger capacity will be 96 and 105, named *Robert the Bruce* and *Sir William Wallace*.

Tugs

Name	Year	PAX	NRT	GRT	LOA	BM	DFT	SPD
Barracuda Bay	1970	Nil	—	—	13.2	3.9	1.7	9
Beaver Bay	1978	Nil	—	41	16.1	4.8	1.7	9

There are also five mooring launches (7.5-9m length) for mooring vessels.

CLYDE SHIPPING CO LTD

132 Cathcart Street, Greenock PA15 1BQ
Tel: (0475-) 20281/28884 *Telex:* 778357

Claiming to be the oldest steamship company in the world, Clyde Shipping Co was founded in Glasgow in 1815 for the purpose of transporting goods between Greenock, Port Glasgow and the City of Glasgow via the Clyde. Short-sea, and coastwise passenger cargo services were started in 1820 and developed into a wide network of regular liner trades until passengers ceased to be carried in 1952. Regular cargo services were terminated in 1968 but deep-sea cargo services were operated from time to time. The company now concentrates on Clyde towage services, a service which has run consistently since 1818, and has over the years taken over Lawson-Batey Tugs and Glenlight Shipping and other interests and has a part share in Forth Tugs Ltd and Shetland Towage Ltd.

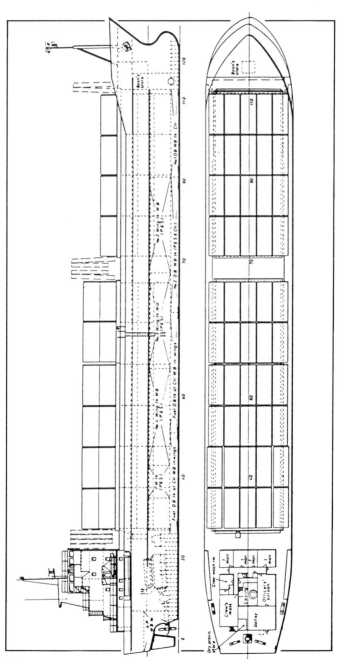

Above:
Commodore Enterprise a typical short-sea gearless containership.
Courtesy: Commodore Shipping

40

Name	Year	NRT	GRT	LOA	BM	DFT	SPD	BP
Flying Childers	1976	Nil	326	38.1	9.2	4	14	35
Flying Fulmar (1)	1974	Nil	298	38.2	9	4	14	37
Flying Phantom (1)	1981	Nil	347	38	9.3	3.8	13	35
Flying Spindrift (2)	1986	77	259	30.7	9	3.4	13	40

Notes: (1) Fitted with fire-fighting equipment; (2) Aquamaster propulsion.

COMMODORE SHIPPING CO LTD

PO Box 10, Commodore House, Buliver Avenue, St Sampson, Guernsey
Tel: (0481) 46841   *Telex:* 4191289

Dating from 1954, Commodore Shipping has grown to be the largest shipping company based in the Channel Islands. The company is involved in container cargo services linking the islands with Belgian, Dutch and UK ports, as well as inter-island passenger and cargo services. Commodore was early to realise the potential of high speed passenger craft and in 1987 introduced a successful summer service with this type of vessel between the islands and Weymouth, which is to be revived in summer 1988. On occasion, the company finds it necessary to charter extra tonnage for its own cargo services; equally, its ships are often out on charter to other operators.

Cargo Ships

Name	Year	NRT	GRT	DWT	LOA	BM	DFT	SPD	TEU
Commodore Clipper	1970	481.6	757.6	1,320	78.5	11.9	4	12.5	62
Commodore Enterprise (1)	1977	937.1	1,246	2,884	95.2	13.6	4.9	13	135
Commodore Goodwill	1985	1,100.2	1,598.2	4,500	97	17.6	6	13	356
Island Commodore	1971	406	588.6	1,427	79	11.1	4.1	12	55
Norman Commodore	1979	406	588.6	1,427	79	11.1	4.1	12	55

Notes: (1) Currently under charter to Norwegian operators. All ships are gearless.

Passenger Craft (no vehicle capacity)

Operated by subsidiary company Condor Ltd on services between Guernsey and other Channel Islands, St Malo and Weymouth (not in winter).

Name	Year	NRT	GRT	LOA	BM	SPD	PAX
Condor 4 (1)	1974	66	129	28.7	6.1	33	136
Condor 5 (1)	1976	83	174	31	6.2	35	180
Condor 7 (1)	1985	128.9	208	31	6.7	36	200
To be named (2)	1988	—	—	33	9.4	32	252

Notes: (1) Hydrofoils; (2) Marinteknik '33' water jet catamaran on charter for 1988 Weymouth summer season.

CORY TOWAGE LTD

Windsor House, 1270 London Road, London SW16 4XH
Tel: (01-) 679 8811   *Telex:* 946941

Wm Cory & Son Ltd first became involved in tug operations on the takeover of the Rea Brothers' business in Liverpool and Bristol (see under Rea Towing Co) in 1918. In 1963, the Bristol subsidiary known as R & J. H. Rea Ltd since 1920, took over towage duties at Cardiff and Barry from the British Transport Docks Board. Between 1969 and 1971 several takeover bids were successful, bringing into the group J. Cooper Ltd of Belfast, Steele & Bennie Ltd of Glasgow and the Newport

Below:
Commodore Shipping *Commodore Goodwill* before gold lions were fixed to the funnel. *Courtesy: Commodore*

Bottom:
Condor *Condor 7*. *Courtesy: Commodore*

Above:
Cory Towage *Point Gilbert*.   *Courtesy: Cory Towage*

Below:
Cory Towage *Eskgarth*.   *Courtesy: M. J. Gaston*

Screw Towing Co Ltd. In 1971 R & J. H. Rea Ltd was reformed as Cory Ship Towage Ltd.

1972 was almost equally active, a joint takeover with Clyde Shipping of the Grangemouth & Forth Towing Co Ltd, was achieved, and in the same year Wm Cory & Son Ltd and its subsidiary companies were themselves taken over by Ocean Transport & Trading Ltd, Liverpool. The firm of W. H. Reynolds, Plymouth, was acquired in 1973, by which time the company was already established in Milford Haven, Bantry Bay and Halifax, Nova Scotia. Shetland Towing Ltd, a Cory joint venture, was set up in 1978, while in 1983 the company succeeded in moving in on Bristol by acquiring C. J. King of Avonmouth, forming Cory King Towage Ltd. At the end of 1985, Cory Ship Towage Ltd was re-styled Cory Towage Ltd. This company now operates British registered tugs at Plymouth, in the Bristol Channel, at Milford Haven, on the Mersey (see Rea Towing Co Ltd), on the Clyde and at Belfast. Overseas towage activities are usually undertaken by non-British vessels.

Plymouth area base (Tel: [0752] 812 238)

Name	Year	GRT	LOA	BM	DFT	SPD	BP
Avongarth	1960	156	29.4	7.6	3.3	12	13.5
Torgarth	1958	13	12.3	3.3	2.1	10	4
Tregarth	1961	13	12.3	3.3	2.1	10	4

Avonmouth and Bristol: Cory King Towage (Tel: [0272] 822 021)

Name	Year	GRT	LOA	BM	DFT	SPD	BP
Lowgarth	1965	152	29	7.6	3.8	12.	15
Pengarth	1962	160	28.7	7.9	3.6	12	14.5
Point Gilbert (1)	1972	334	39.4	9.6	3.7	13	45
Point James (1)	1972	334	39.4	9.6	3.7	13	36
Sea Challenge	1967	185	31	8.2	3.7	12	22
Sea Endeavour	1980	213	31	9	4.6	14	42

South Wales: Newport and Barry (Tel: [0633] 56835)

Name	Year	GRT	LOA	BM	DFT	SPD	BP
Bargarth	1966	161	28.9	7.6	3.7	12	17
Butegarth	1966	161	28.9	7.6	3.7	12	17
Danegarth	1966	161	29	7.6	3.7	12	14
Emsgarth	1975	159	28.5	7.3	4	13	26
Gwentgarth	1972	156	28.5	7.8	4.2	13	21
Hallgarth (2)	1979	204	28.4	8.9	4.5	13	23.5
Holmgarth (2)	1979	204	28.4	8.9	4.5	13	23.5
Uskgarth	1966	161	29	7.6	3.7	12	14

Milford Haven (Tel: [06462] 2296)

Name	Year	GRT	LOA	BM	DFT	SPD	BP
Edengarth	1976	381	37.9	10.8	4.9	12.5	49
Eskgarth	1976	381	37.9	10.8	4.9	12.5	49
Exegarth	1976	388	37.9	10.8	4.9	12.5	49
Eyegarth (1)	1977	388	37.9	10.8	4.9	12.5	49
Glengarth (1)	1970	291	39	9.1	4.3	12	35
Graygarth (1)	1970	291	39.3	8.9	4.3	12	35
Greengarth (1)	1970	291	39	9.1	4.3	12	35

Clyde (Tel: [0475] 23266)

Name	Year	GRT	LOA	BM	DFT	SPD	BP
Campaigner (3)	1965	306	38.7	9.1	4.3	12	22
Chieftain	1968	205	34.2	8.8	4	12	27
Point Spencer	1973	366	39.4	9.6	3.7	12.5	40
Thunderer	1970	272	38	9.8	4.3	12	38

Belfast (Tel: [0232] 743278)

Name	Year	GRT	LOA	BM	DFT	SPD	BP
Clandeboye (1)	1967	167	30	8	3.8	12	20
Coleraine (1)	1970	212	32.2	8.9	4.3	12	32.5
Craigdarragh	1966	169	30	8	3.8	11	14.5

Below:
Cory Towage *Hallgarth*.   *Courtesy: M. J. Gaston*

Name	Year	GRT	LOA	BM	DFT	SPD	BP
Dunosprey	1968	173	30.4	8.3	4	11	22

Notes: (1) Fitted with fire-fighting equipment; (2) Voith Schneider propulsion; (3) transferred to Foynes

CUNARD LINE LTD
30/35 Pall Mall, London SW1Y 5LS
Tel: (01-) 930 4321   *Telex:* 295483

Although, like some cargo ships, Cunard's passenger ships are technically owned by the Cunard Steam-Ship Co, they are controlled and operated totally separately by Cunard Line Ltd. Operations are centred on the *QE2's* trans-Atlantic crossings, and cruises world-wide by her and other members of the fleet. In addition to the two listed below, also owned are *Cunard Princess, Sagafjord* and *Vistfjord*, registered in the Bahamas, and *Sea Goddess I* and *Sea Goddess II*, registered in Norway. They are not therefore British flag ships.

Name	Year	NRT	GRT	LOA	BM	DFT	SPD	PAX
Cunard Countess	1976	10,140	17,593	163	23	18.7	19	750
Queen Elizabeth 2	1968	37,471	69,053	293.5	32	9.9	28	1,850

THE CUNARD-ELLERMAN SHIPPING SERVICES DEPARTMENT
20 Eastbourne Terrace, Paddington, London W2 6LE
Tel: (01-) 258 3738   *Telex:* 27602

This organisation was founded specifically to manage the combined cargo fleets of Ellerman Lines and Cunard following the merger of Ellerman with the latter in June 1987. The new department is now responsible for Cunard's oil tankers, interests in Atlantic Container Line and the CAMEL (Cunard Arabia Middle East Lines) consortium, as well as Ellerman's Iberian and Mediterranean operations. The merger also effectively gives Cunard control of ACT(A) with a combined ownership of 57½% in the seven containerships *ACT-1* to *ACT-7*, and now Ellerman's 65.6% interest in *ACT-8*, in which Harrison has the remainder.

Although Cunard's history, as one of Britain's oldest and leading shipping companies over the years, has been well publicised, it is worth mentioning here that financial difficulties led directly to the absorption by Trafalgar House in 1971. Ellerman's background is less well known. Founded relatively recently, this company can be said to have its origins in 1892, when John R. Ellerman gained control of his first shipping company. After that the Ellerman Empire grew quickly, many other companies falling into its control including the City Line, Hall Line, Wilson Line and Westcott & Laurance, to name but a few. Family control of the company ceased in 1983, when Shirespell Ltd (a hotel and leisure orientated concern) took over, and this was followed by a management buy-out two years later.

Name	Year	NRT	GRT	DWT	LOA	BMD	DFT	SPD	TEU
Atlantic Conveyor (1)	1984	21,660	58,438	35,626	295.1	32.3	9.8	17	2,911
City of Lisbon (2)	1979	1,064	1,599	4,352	104.1	16.8	5.7	15	300
City of Plymouth (2)	1978	1,084	1,599	4,352	104.1	16.8	5.7	15	300
Liverpool Star (2)	1979	1,083	1,599	4,352	104.1	16.8	5.7	15	300
Lucerna (3)	1975	17,030	23,736	39,865	182.9	32.3	11.4	15	Nil

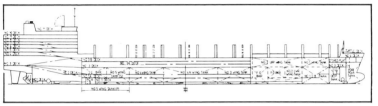

Top:
Cunard Steamship Co *Atlantic Conveyor*. *Courtesy: Cunard/Geo Gibson*

Above:
Cunard's 'stretched' deep-sea/container ro-ro vessel *Atlantic Conveyor*.
Courtesy: Cunard

Below:
Cunard Steamship Co *Lumiere* *Courtesy: Fotoflite*

Top:
Ellerman Lines *City of Plymouth*.   Courtesy: Fotoflite

Above:
Dover Harbour Board *Deft*.   Courtesy: Dover Harbour Board

Below:
Esso *Esso Avon*.   Courtesy: Esso Petroleum

Name	Year	NRT	GRT	DWT	LOA	BMD	DFT	SPD	TEU
Lumiere (3)	1972	9,630	14,924	24,951	169.6	24.7	9.5	14	Nil
Luminetta (3)	1972	9,630	14,924	24,951	169.1	24.7	9.5	14	Nil

Notes: (1) Trans-Atlantic ro-ro container ships; (2) tonnage engaged in Iberian and Mediterranean services; (3) oil tankers, world-wide trading.

Also associated with Cunard-Ellerman Shipping Services Department under the overall control of Cunard Cargo Ltd is Ellerman City Liners PLC of 12-20 Camomile Street, London EC3 7EX, with part ownership of deep-sea containerships *Benalder*, *Benavon* and *City of Edinburgh* (see under Ben Line Steamers).

Both Cunard and Ellerman entities charter in outside tonnage where necessary respectively for CAMEL and Mediterranean services, while Ellerman owns some Bahamaian-flag vessels.

DOVER HARBOUR BOARD

Harbour House, Marine Parade, Dover, Kent CT17 9BU
Tel: (0304) 240400   *Telex:* 965619

Dover Harbour Board was founded by Royal Charter of King James I in 1606. Tug operations started in the 1820s, when sailing ships were the only customers. Since then, tugs have constantly been in operation, both for assisting in the berthing of cross-channel ferries in inclement weather (the first steam packets started using the port in the early 1830s) and for aiding ships in the channel. Current operations maintain this pattern. Both tugs are equipped with fire-fighting facilities, and are of the tractor type fitted with Voith Schneider propellers.

Name	Year	GRT	LOA	BM	DFT	SPD	BP
Deft	1984	287	29.9	9	4.5	12	29
Dextrous	1984	287	29.9	9	4.5	12	29

ESSO PETROLEUM CO LTD

Supply & Transportation Department, Administration Building, Fawley, Southampton SO4 1TX
Tel: (0703) 892033   *Telex:* 24942

Part of the Exxon Group, Esso Petroleum Co has its origins in the registration in London of the Anglo-American Oil Co Ltd in 1888, set up to import and market American oils. In 1947 Esso Transportation Co Ltd was formed to operate the shipping side, but in 1951 (when the Fawley refinery was opened), responsibility for the fleet was transferred to Anglo-American, which was renamed Esso Petroleum Co Ltd. All types of oil products are carried coastwise, within Europe and world-wide.

Name	Year	NRT	GRT	DWT	LOA	BM	DFT	SPD
Esso Aberdeen	1967	42,595	59,268	111,052	276.5	41.4	14.8	17.5
Esso Avon	1981	984	1,599	3,122	91.2	13	5.5	12
Esso Clyde	1972	6,890	12,317	20,448	166.5	22.85	9.2	15.5
Esso Demetia	1973	98,678	125,293	254,890	340.5	51.9	20.1	15.8
Esso Fawley	1967	5,999	11,046	18,377	163.6	22	8.5	15.5
Esso Inverness	1971	930	2,178	3,430	91.4	12.8	5.9	13.8
Esso Mersey	1972	6,802	12,323	20,510	166.6	22.8	9.2	15.6
Esso Milford Haven	1967	6,239	10,902	18,377	163.7	22	8.7	16.8

Above:
Esso Petroleum's Esso Plymouth.
Courtesy: Cochrane Shipbuilders

Below:
Esso Esso Severn. Courtesy: Esso Petroleum/Skyfotos

Name	Year	NRT	GRT	DWT	LOA	BM	DFT	SPD
Esso Penzance	1971	930	2,178	3,404	91.4	13.3	5.9	13.8
Esso Plymouth	1980	821	1,421	2,162	70.8	12.7	4.5	11.8
Esso Severn	1975	6,890	12,317	20,449	166.6	22.8	9.2	15.5
Esso Tees	1970	8,317	12,683	21,116	170.1	23.5	9.4	13.8
Esso Tenby	1970	930	2,170	3,430	91.4	12.8	5.9	13.8
Esso Warwickshire	1962	32,464	48,049	84,688	263.2	34.3	15	16

F. T. EVERARD & SONS LTD

14/20 St Mary Axe, London EC3A 8BL
Tel: (01-) 623 8088   *Telex:* 887230

Celebrating its centenary in 1980, the family firm of Everards was founded at Greenhithe on the Thames. It was originally a ship-building yard. Trading started in 1893 with the purchase of the sailing barge named *Industry*. The first motor vessel in the fleet was the *Grit* built at Greenhithe in 1912. Since then, the company has expanded into road haulage, Thames lighterage, insurance, chartering and ship management. In postwar years a number of other well known companies have been acquired including J. Wharton, Keadby in 1952 and Comben Longstaff in 1980. The company specialises in the movement of dry and liquid bulk cargoes, timber and steel, mainly in North European waters. The company became established in the liner trade between Ireland, the UK and Scandinavia — which still operates — on the takeover of Glen & Co Ltd, Glasgow, in 1961.

Name	Year	NRT	GRT	DWT	LOA	BM	DFT
Ability (1)	1979	860	1,490	2,551	79.3	13.2	2
Activity (1)	1969	394	697	1,356	74	10.4	4
Allurity (1)	1969	394	697	1,356	74	10.4	4
Amenity (1)	1980	883	1,453	2,528	79.3	13.2	5
Asperity (1)	1967	402	698	1,326	71.9	9.9	3.8
Audacity (1)	1968	460	699	1,616	72.6	11.1	4.4
Authenticity (1)	1979	860	1,409	2,551	79.3	13.2	5
Candourity (3)	1975	330	499	888	56.2	9.9	3.2
Capacity (3)	1980	554	798	1,315	60.4	11.3	3.9
Celebrity (3)	1976	367	582	947	57.6	10	3.3
City (3)	1976	330	499	888	56.2	9.9	3.2
Comity (3)	1980	554	798	1,315	60.4	11.3	3.9
Commodity (3)	1975	367	582	947	57.6	10	3.3
Conformity (3)	1975	330	499	888	56.2	9.9	3.2
Lancasterbrook (3)	1975	1,067	1,599	3,700	93.1	13.7	5.6
Leicesterbrook (2)	1977	1,118	1,599	3,619	93.6	13.7	5.6
Mairi Everard (3)	1974	1,027	1,599	2,638	77.6	13.2	5
Pamela Everard (3)	1984	545	799	2,415	79	12.7	4.6
Sagacity (3)	1973	1,162	1,595	3,238	91.3	13.3	5.1
Sanguity (3)	1984	545	799	2,415	79	12.7	4.6
Selectivity (3)	1984	545	799	2,415	79	12.7	4.6
Sociality (3)	1986	545	799	2,415	79	12.7	4.6
Speciality (3)	1977	1,053	1,597	4,554	91.1	14.3	6.3
Stability (3)	1978	1,053	1,597	4,554	91.1	14.3	6.4

Notes: (1) Tankers; (2) geared dry bulk cargo; (3) gearless dry cargo.

Right:
Everard Stability.   *Courtesy: Everard/Skyfotos*

Top:
Everard *Authenticity*.   Courtesy: Everard/Skyfotos

Above:
Everard *Capacity* as *Lizzonia*.   Courtesy: Everard/Skyfotos

Above:
Falmouth Towage *St Eval*. Courtesy: Falmouth Towage

Below:
James Fisher *Aberthaw Fisher*. Author

Bottom:
Coe-Metcalf *Frank M*. Courtesy: Fotoflite

THE FALMOUTH TOWAGE CO LTD

The Docks, Falmouth, Cornwall TR11 4NR
Tel: (0326) 311 400   *Telex:* 45536

Founded in 1931 from predecessors dating back to the last century. Between 1918 and 1977 it was a member of the P&O group, along with Falmouth Dockyard, both being part of the Silley, Cox & Co organisation. In 1977 British Shipbuilders took over, until privatisation in 1985 when Falmouth Towage and the dockyard changed hands again, being bought by Cuehold plc. Taken over in 1987 with the drydock company by Highland Participants. The company specialises in harbour and estuary towage.

Name	Year	GRT	LOA	BM	DFT	BP	SPD
St Budoc	1958	208	31.6	8.5	4.5	22	10
St Eval	1960	187	2.7	8	4	11	22
St Gluvius	1959	207	32.4	8.5	4.5	20	10
St Piran	1960	306	39.1	9.1	4.8	22	10

JAMES FISHER & SONS PLC

PO Box 4, Fisher House, Barrow-in-Furness, Cumbria LA14 1HR
Tel: (0229) 22323   *Telex:* 65163

Founded in 1847, Fishers have long been associated with the operation of short-sea coasters, particularly in the dry-bulk and general cargo trades. Over the years, the company's strength has been demonstrated by the take-over of other companies, notably Coe-Metcalf (formed in 1935 on the merger of S. W. Coe and Metcalf Motor Coasters) and Northern Ireland's Shamrock Shipping Co Ltd (established in 1897) among other interests. The company also manages ships on behalf of others, and charters out owned ships to a variety of operators. Anchorage Ferrying Services Ltd, another subsidiary, was formed in 1968. Some group ships are registered under non-UK flags — these are therefore not included below.

James Fisher & Sons plc

Name	Year	NRT	GRT	DWT	LOA	BM	DFT	SPD
Aberthaw Fisher (1)	1966	835	2,355	2,233	86.6	16.5	4.6	11
Darnia (3)	1978	1,636	3,455	1,791	114.4	18.1	4.6	—
Kingsnorth Fisher (1)	1966	835	2,355	2,233	86.7	16.5	4.6	11
Loch Awe (4)	1971	771	1,537	2,517	82.2	12.1	3.7	12
Peveril (5)	1977	684	1,976	1,929	106.3	16	5	14

Notes: (1) Managed for the Central Electricity Generating Board and specially built for carrying heavy loads (up to 700 tonnes) by ro-ro method for servicing power stations; (2) geared dry cargo; (3) ro-ro ship on charter to Sealink British Ferries; (4) dry cargo gearless; (5) ro-ro ship on charter to Isle of Man Steam Packet Co Ltd.
Also owned is *Atlantic Fisher* (1976; 5,482), laid up.

Anchorage Ferrying Services Ltd, Barrow

Name	Year	NRT	GRT	DWT	LOA	BM	DFT	SPD
Odin (1)	1968	1,378	1,844	3,434	73.8	12.5	5.7	8.5
Scafell (2)	1971	781	1,537	2,515	82.2	12.1	4.4	12.5

Notes: (1) Sea-going barge; (2) dry cargo carrier.

Above:
Coe-Metcalf *Quickthorn*.   *Courtesy: Fotoflite*

Below:
Shamrock Shipping *David Dorman*.   *Courtesy: Fotoflite*

Bottom:
Forth Tugs *Kelty*.   *Courtesy: M. J. Gaston*

Coe Metcalf Shipping Ltd, Liverpool

Name	Year	NRT	GRT	DWT	LOA	BM	DFT	SPD
Firethorn (1)	1967	611	1,041	1,707	67.1	11.2	4.6	12
Frank M (2)	1965	579	1,307	1,819	70.7	11.4	4.8	11
Frederick M (2)	1980	872	1,594	2,924	75.2	13.3	5.8	12
Gorsethorn (3)	1963	705	1,569	2,023	83.8	12.2	5.1	11
Hawthorn (1)	1967	679	1,026	1,735	75.8	11.1	4.4	12
John M (2)	1963	588	1,308	1,839	70.7	11.4	4.8	10
Nicholas M (2)	1965	579	1,308	1,819	70.7	11.4	4.8	10
Pholas (4)	1958	1,628	3,775	3,997	99.1	15.3	7	10
Quickthorn (1)	1967	869	1,598	2,481	85.4	12.9	4.9	13
Robert M (5)	1970	749	1,593	2,449	85	12.8	4.4	11
Whitehorn (6)	1963	759	—	2,023	79.6	12.2	5.1	14

Notes: (1) Dry cargo carrier; (2) tanker; (3) geophysical survey vessel; (4) self-positioning drill ship; (5) bitumen tanker; (6) drill ship.

Shamrock Shipping Co Ltd, Belfast

Name	Year	NRT	GRT	DWT	LOA	BM	DFT	SPD
David Dorman	1978	394	664	953	57.5	10.1	3.4	11
Edgar Dorman	1978	393	664	953	57.5	10.1	3.4	11
Shamrock Endeavour	1982	652	995	1,694	69.4	10.7	4.3	10
Shamrock Enterprise	1982	652	995	1,694	69.4	10.7	4.3	10

All the above are gearless dry cargo carriers.

FORTH TUGS LTD

PO Box 12, Grangemouth, Stirlingshire FK3 8BR
Tel: (0324) 482 401

Originally incorporated from the merger of the Grangemouth Towing Co and Forth Towing in 1895. The name was changed in 1972 to Forth Tugs Ltd following the purchase of the company by Clyde Shipping Co and Cory Ship Towage, each with 50% of the shares. At the same time, the company concentrated its activities at Grangemouth and the Hound Point Oil Terminal, abandoning operations at other Forth ports.

Name	Year	GRT	LOA	BM	DFT	BP	SPD
Almond	1976	322	38	9.2	4.6	36	14
Boquhan (1)	1975	326	37.3	9.2	4.8	39	14
Carron (1, 2)	1979	210	28.1	8.5	4.5	25	12
Duchray (1)	1975	326	37.3	9.2	4.8	39	14
Forth (1, 2)	1979	210	28.1	8.5	4.5	25	12
Kelty	1976	322	38	9.2	4.6	36	14

Notes: (1) Fitted with fire-fighting equipment; (2) Voith Schneider propulsion. All tugs have anti-pollution capability.

FURNESS WITHY SHIPPING LTD

Furness House, 53 Brighton Road, Redhill, Surrey RH1 6YL
Tel: (0737) 771122   *Telex:* 0850701

Formed in 1891, Furness Withy was to develop into one of the leading British shipping groups. Over the years many famous names such as Houlder, Prince Line and Shaw Savill were absorbed, followed more recently by Royal Mail Lines and the Pacific Steam Navigation Co in 1965. In 1980 the Furness Withy Group

Above left:
Furness Withy *Abbey*. *Courtesy: Fotoflite*

Left:
Furness Withy *Andes*. *Courtesy: Fotoflite*

Below left:
Furness Withy *Manchester Challenge*. *Courtesy: Fotoflite*

Above:
J. & A. Gardner *Saint Brandan*. *Courtesy: Fotoflite*

Below:
Geest Line *Geestport*. *Courtesy: Fotoflite*

itself was taken over by the Orient Overseas (Holdings) Ltd of Hong Kong (C. Y. Tung), who shortly after also acquired Manchester Liners and in 1983 Dart Containerline. The company now manages and operates ships on liner services to the Mediterranean, Canada, Central and South America and East Coast USA. Subsidiary Furness Withy (Agencies) Ltd acts as UK agents for all OO(H) companies.

Name	Year	NRT	GRT	DWT	LOA	BM	DFT	SPD	TEU
Abbey (1)	1979	44,023	64,154	118,750	263.7	40.8	15.9	16	Nil
Andes (2)	1984	18,016	32,016	37,042	202.5	32.3	12	20	2,145
British Steel (3)	1984	58,786	90,831	173,028	286.9	47	17.8	14	Nil
Canadian Explorer (4)	1978	15,762	26,051	33,869	218.6	31.1	11.8	23	1,737
Manchester Challenge (4)	1970	13,384	30,817	28,488	231.5	30.6	10.1	22	1,852

Notes: (1) Gearless bulk carrier; (2) geared vessel engaged in West Coast South American liner service; (3) gearless bulk carrier managed for British Steel; (4) engaged in liner service to/from St Lawrence, gearless.
From 1 July 1988 the North Atlantic container service operated by Dart/Manchester Liners is re-styled OOCL (see also Island Navigation p68).

J. & A. GARDNER & CO LTD

228 Clyde Street, Glasgow G1 4JS
Tel: (041-) 221 7845   *Telex:* 77205

Established in 1895, Gardners have specialised in the carriage of coal on UK coastal voyages and to Ireland. The decline in the coal trade led to diversification, and apart from one chemical tanker, the fleet now consist of bow-ramp loading ro-ro ferries for handling heavy goods, mostly between UK and Irish ports.

Name	Year	NRT	GRT	DWT	LOA	BM	DFT	SPD
Saint Angus	1980	611	943	1,452	64.7	11.2	3.8	12
Saint Brandan	1976	501	931	1,394	63.8	10.8	4.1	12
Saint Kearan (1)	1978	180	441	775	50.4	9.1	3.3	9
Saint Oran	1981	330	573	720	53.3	9.2	3.4	10

Note: (1) Chemical tanker

THE GEEST LINE LTD

Windward Terminal, No 3 Dock, PO Box 20, Barry CF6 8XE
Tel: (0446-) 700 333   *Telex:* 498359

Geest's dedicated banana service between the West Indies and the UK started operating into Preston in 1953 with chartered ships. Ship owning followed later as trade built up. The UK terminal was transferred to the Bristol Channel in 1972 and the service now operates on a weekly basis from Barry to the Windward Islands. The company is unusual in offering passenger accommodation, the older pair having cabins for eight, the others for twelve. All ships are fully geared.

Name	Year	NRT	GRT	DWT	LOA	BM	DFT	SPD
Geestbay	1981	4,445	7,729	9,970	159.1	21.3	8.8	19
Geestcape	1975	5,185	10,397	11,168	157.3	22.6	9.4	21.5
Geesthaven	1975	16,115	10,397	11,168	157.3	22.6	9.4	21.5
Geestport	1982	4,445	7,729	9,970	159.1	21.3	8.8	19

GEORGE GIBSON & CO LTD

16 Bernard Street, Leith, Edinburgh EH6 6QA
Tel: (031-) 554 4466   *Telex:* 727492

The ships operated and managed by Gibson are all liquid gas carriers, and are owned by Anchor Line Ltd. Gibson was taken over by the Runciman Group in 1972, Anchor Line having been a wholly owned subsidiary since 1965. They are engaged in mainly European trading.

Name	Year	NRT	GRT	DWT	LOA	BM	DFT	SPD
Borthwick	1977	1,105	1,596	2,104	78.9	73.2	5.3	13
Heriot	1972	963	1,584	2,594	78.1	12.9	6.2	14
Melrose	1971	1,298	1,999	2,713	86.9	13.2	6.1	14
Quentin	1977	1,165	1,597	2,090	75.7	69.6	5.2	14
Traquair	1981	2,977	5,967	7,230	106.5	18.3	8.1	16

GILLIE & BLAIR LTD

Proctor House, Newcastle upon Tyne NE1 3JJ
Tel: (091-) 232 3431   *Telex:* 53344

Founded in 1911, Gillie & Blair specialise in the management and operation of coastal and middle distance cargo ships, mainly on a tramp basis. Apart from the *Wimpey Geocore*, which is a drill ship, all others are general dry cargo carriers.

Name	Year	NRT	GRT	DWT	LOA	BM	DFT	SPD
Ardent	1981	372	498	1,180	55	9.4	3.6	9
Marianne Norcoast	1971	233	396	1,016	59.3	10.6	3.6	10
Millac Star II	1974	359	500	1,570	75.5	11.8	3.9	12
Wimpey Geocore (1)	1963	958	1,545	2,489	85.2	12	5.2	11

Notes: (1) Is a converted F. T. Everard cargo ship 1982

GLENLIGHT SHIPPING LTD

Winton Pier, The Harbour, Ardrossan KA22 8EE
Tel: (0294) 605115   *Telex:* 777853

A member of the Clyde Shipping Group of Companies, Glenlight was formed in 1968 on the amalgamation of the last two operators of traditional 'puffers', Hay, Hamilton Ltd and Ross & Marshall Ltd. The ships trade mostly in the Irish Sea and West of Scotland carrying dry bulk and general cargoes, and are fitted with 2 to 5 tonnes travelling gantry cranes.

Name	Year	NRT	GRT	DWT	LOA	BM	DFT	SPD
Glencloy	1974	358	499	770	53.5	9.6	3.2	9
Glenetive	1970	147	199	429	41.7	7.6	3	8
Glenrosa	1969	147	199	429	41.7	7.6	3	8
Pibroch	1957	52	99	160	26.5	6.1	2.9	8
Polarlight	1970	147	199	424	41.7	7.6	3	8
Sealight	1970	147	199	429	41.7	7.6	3	8

Above:
George Gibson & Co *Heriot*. *Courtesy: Fotoflite*

Below:
Glenlight *Glencloy*. *Courtesy: Glenlight Shipping*

Bottom:
T. & J. Harrison *Author*. *Courtesy: Fotoflite*

GRAIG SHIPPING PLC (Idwal Williams & Co Ltd; Managers)

113-116 Bute Street, Cardiff CF1 6TE
Tel: (0222) 488636   Telex: 498527

Born in the coal boom at the end of World War 1, the company bought its first steamship in 1919 and has traded in dry bulk cargoes ever since. Since 1971, the firm has diversified into other activities, including taking interests in oil exploration by the setting up of Graig Exploration Ltd and in wells in Ohio. Gearless ships are engaged in world-wide tramping.

Name	Year	NRT	GRT	DWT	LOA	BM	DFT	SPD
Graiglas	1974	40,019	57,255	109,880	254.5	40.8	14.8	15.5
Graigwerdd (1)	1982	14,895	22,474	38,095	201.5	27.9	11.8	16.5

Note: (1) A second vessel of a similar size is due to be delivered late in 1988.

THOS & JAS HARRISON LTD

Mersey Chambers, 5 Old Church Yard, Liverpool L2 8UF
Tel: (051-) 236 6511   Telex: 628404

The 'Harrison Line' as the company became known, is considered to have been founded in 1853, when the two brothers, Thomas and James took full control of the Liverpool shipping company George Brown & Harrison, for which both had previously worked. The first steamship, the *Philosopher* was acquired in 1857. From continental trading, the company quickly expanded, establishing liner services over the years to India, the Caribbean and Southern Africa, among others. The Charente Steam-Ship Co Ltd was formed in 1884 to take over the steamship business, Thos and Jas Harrison becoming the managers. The last sailing ship was sold in 1887. Diversification into bulk carrying dates from 1973. Owned container vessels now operate within the CAROL (Caribbean Overseas Lines) consortium.

Name	Year	NRT	GRT	DWT	LOA	BM	DFT	SPD	TEU
Adviser (1)	1977	15,343	27,867	27,893	204	31	10	22	1,412
Author	1981	13,241	27,994	27,631	204	31	10	22	1,412
Warrior (2)	1973	10,482	16,317	27,571	174.1	23	10.9	15	—

Notes: (1) On charter to Cie Generale Maritime as *CGM Provence*. The company has about 34% share in *ACT 8* (see ACT[A]), Ellerman holding the balance; (2) dry bulk carrier.

HAYS MARINE SERVICES LTD

11-13 Canal Road, Rochester, Kent ME2 4DS
Tel: (0634) 290092   Telex: 96276

Dating from 1985, Hays Marine Services Ltd is a holding company which owns two well known companies, Bowker & King Ltd, London (founded in 1884) and Crescent Shipping, Rochester (1907). The former specialises in the carriage of oils and other liquids, while Crescent is most closely associated with dry bulk cargoes. Both operate on coastwise, estuary and near continental trades, though from time to time longer voyages are undertaken. Ship management and chartering also form an active part of the group operations. The group was the subject of a UK

Top:
T. & J. Harrison *Warrior*. *Courtesy: Fotoflite*

Above:
Bowker & King *Beckenham*. *Courtesy: Fotoflite*

Below:
Crescent Shipping *Ambience*. *Courtesy: Fotoflite*

management buy-out from former owners, Kuwait Investment Office, late in 1987.

Bowker & King Ltd (all ships are tankers)

Name	Year	NRT	GRT	DWT	LOA	BM	DFT	SPD
Banwell	1980	522	999	2,000	72	11.1	3.7	10.5
Bardsey	1981	613	1,144	1,767	69.5	11.8	4.3	11
Barmouth	1980	679	1,100	1,771	69.5	11.8	4.3	11
Barrier (1)	1958	229	487	508	52.4	10.4	2.5	6.5
Beckenham	1980	540	825	1,165	64.2	11.5	3.3	9.5
Beckton	1971	115	239	339	39.9	6.7	2.5	9
Beechcroft	1966	316	615	833	53.7	10.2	3.1	9
Berkeley	1969	332	730	1,219	64.6	9.2	3.7	10
Bisley	1969	345	701	1,290	64.3	9.2	3.8	11
Blackfriars	1985	525	992	1,650	69.9	11.3	3.8	9.6
Blackheath	1980	431	751	1,098	60	11.3	3.7	11
Blakeley	1971	363	728	1,229	64.3	9.3	3.8	10
Borman	1969	338	730	1,219	64.6	9.2	3.7	10
Botley	1950	57	105	120	27	6	1.9	5
Bouncer	1968	97	209	330	35	7.5	2.3	8.5
Breaksea	1985	525	992	1,650	69.9	11.3	3.8	9.6
Brentwood	1980	542	994	1,640	69.8	11.3	3.8	9
Bristolian	1969	533	899	1,321	64.8	11.1	3.4	10
Bromley	1978	343	640	844	57.2	11.2	2.9	10.5
Bude	1971	363	728	1,229	64.3	9.3	3.8	10
Budleigh	1969	332	730	1,219	64.5	9.2	3.7	10

Notes: (1) Rebuilt 1982.
Bowker & King's tankers usually work on the Thames, Solent and Bristol Channel.

Crescent Shipping Ltd (owned, gearless, dry cargo vessels)

Name	Year	NRT	GRT	DWT	LOA	BM	DFT	SPD
Ambience	1983	336.1	492.8	840	50	9.2	3.3	9
Boisterence	1983	262	536	830	50	9.2	3.4	9
Crescence	1982	336.1	492.8	840	50	9.2	3.3	9
Insistence	1975	269.3	474.7	747	50	8.8	3.2	9
Jubilence	1975	269.3	474.7	747	50	8.8	3.2	9
Kindrence	1976	1,134.3	1,595.6	3,210	91.3	13.3	5.1	12
Luminence (1)	1977	1,134.3	1,595.6	3,210	91.3	13.3	5.1	12
Militence	1978	565.6	959.5	1,408	71.4	11.2	3.3	9.5
Nascence	1978	565.6	959.5	1,408	71.4	11.2	3.3	9.5
Ordinence	1978	270.8	469.6	727	49.1	8.8	3.2	9
Piquence	1979	593.8	945.2	1,453	71.4	11.2	3.3	9.5
Quiescence	1979	593.8	945.2	1,453	71.4	11.2	3.3	9.5
Resilience (2)	1969	458.7	988.3	1,324	66.3	11.3	4.1	11.5
Stridence	1983	439.7	698.9	1,821	84.8	11.4	3.4	10
Tarquence	1980	347.5	499.4	830	50	9.2	3.4	9
Turbulence	1983	439.7	698.9	1,821	84.8	11.4	3.4	10
Urgence	1981	435.2	699.3	1,842	84.8	11.4	3.5	10
Vibrence	1981	435.2	699.3	1,842	84.8	11.4	3.5	10

Notes: (1) Adapted for cable-laying operations; (2) bulk starch carrier. Crescent Shipping also manages several smaller dry cargo vessels owned by individuals in the Rochester, Kent area.

HOLYHEAD TOWING CO LTD

Newry Beach Yard, Holyhead, Gwynedd LL65 1YB
Tel: (0407) 50111   *Telex:* 61179

Founded in Holyhead in the early 1960s with a small boatyard repair facility for pleasure craft, the company quickly expanded to include work on commercial craft like tugs and trawlers. The setting up of a towage and salvage company soon followed. Repair work to large ships at anchor as well as alongside, is now a speciality, as is deep-sea towage, and the group has recently taken over the operation of the 137m dry dock at Holyhead.

Name	Year	GRT	LOA	BM	DFT	BP	SPD
Afon Cefni	1961	36.4	18.7	5.1	2.5	7.5	9
Afon Goch	1967	232	33.5	8.8	5	38	12
Afon Las	1952	159	28.9	7.6	3.8	18	10
Carmel Head	1930*	29	15.1	4.1	2	6	8
North Stack	1930*	29	15.1	4.1	2	6	8

Notes: *Rebuilt 1976.
The company also owns a number of small tug/workboats and pontoons.

HOVERSPEED LTD

Maybrook House, Queen's Gardens, Dover, Kent CT17 9UQ
Tel: (0304) 240241   *Telex:* 96323

Hoverspeed's origins can be traced back to 1966 when its predecessor, Hoverlloyd, started passenger-only services between Ramsgate and Calais. In 1982, the latter became a British Rail subsidiary known as British Rail Hovercraft Ltd, which in turn was taken over by Sea Containers Ltd in June 1986. Although part of the Sealink British Ferries 'sector', the company maintains its operational and administrative independence.

Name	Year	REG	DWT	LOA	BM	SPD	PAX
The Prince of Wales	1977	GH 2054	171	36.6	23.8	45	278
Sir Christopher	1972	GH 2008	171	36.6	23.8	45	278
Swift	1969	GH 2004	171	36.6	23.8	45	278
The Princess Anne	1969	GH 2007	280	56.4	23.8	45	424
The Princess Margaret	1968	GH 2006	280	56.4	23.8	45	424

Notes: (1) The hovercraft operate between Dover and Boulogne and Calais for passengers, cars and light vans. Because they are technically aircraft and not ships they carry an airliner type registration number.

HUDSON STEAMSHIP CO LTD

25 Ship Street, Brighton BN1 1AD
Tel: (0273) 21845   *Telex:* 877900

Hudson Steamship Co Ltd is a member of the Thornhope Group, along with the Thorncliffe Shipping Co Ltd, and Thornhope Ltd, for all of which Hudson act as managers. The company specialises in the carriage of dry bulk and liquid cargoes on a world-wide basis, the group also owns other ships under foreign registration. Taken over by Norway's A/S Mosvald, early this year.

The Thornhope Shipping Co Ltd

Name	Year	NRT	GRT	DWT	LOA	BM	DFT	SPD
Warden Point (1)	1978	2,377	3,895	6,440	105.6	14.9	6.8	12

Notes: (1) On charter to Central Electricity Generating Board, usually carrying coal to Thames and Medway from North East England and the Continent.

ISLAND NAVIGATION CORPORATION (INTERNATIONAL) LTD

Floor 23, Harbour Centre, 25 Harbour Road, Wan Chai, Hong Kong
Tel: (5) 8333111   *Telex:* 73219

Island Navigation is the management company for ships operated by the Orient Overseas Container Line, which started trans-Pacific container services in the late 1960s, and a number of other companies.

OOCL also now operates a container service between the Far East and UK/Europe among others. Many ships are registered in foreign countries, but the following fly the British flag.

Name	Year	NRT	GRT	DWT	LOA	BM	DFT	SPD	TEU
Hong Kong Container	1974	22,685	38,864	35,518	264.5	3.2	12	26	2,068
Oriental Ambassador	1977	9,231	17,385	17,607	168.9	25.2	9.4	19	946
Oriental Chief	1976	24,248	39,505	41,587	270.8	30.7	11.5	22	2,466
Oriental Educator	1978	20,389	36,171	38,743	252.2	30.5	10.4	24	2,394
Oriental Freedom	1985	23,885	40,978	44,452	241	32.3	10.6	20	2,498
Pacific Prestige (1)	1981	25,932	35,840	65,015	224.5	32.3	12.9	15	Nil
Pacific Pride (1)	1981	25,101	37,562	64,919	228	32.3	12.2	15	Nil
Pacific Prominence (1)	1982	25,584	35,627	64,916	224.5	32.3	12.9	15	Nil
Tokyo Bridge	1978	12,106	27,297	24,037	227.6	27.7	10.6	19	1,930

Note: (1) Bulk carriers operating on a world-wide tramp basis.

ISLE OF MAN STEAM PACKET CO LTD

PO Box No 5, Douglas, Isle of Man
Tel: (0624) 233 44   *Telex:* 629414

Founded in Douglas in 1830, to operate passenger and cargo services all year round to and from Liverpool, the company expanded its services rapidly until the 1970s when changing social patterns resulted in fewer people taking Manx holidays. In 1985 the unthinkable happened and the all year round services with Liverpool were withdrawn (although reinstated the following year on an occasional basis), and the company merged with Sealink British Ferries in providing services between Douglas and Heysham. Summer season only links are now maintained between Douglas and Liverpool, Dublin, Belfast, Stranraer and Fleetwood. In 1985, a 40% share in the company was acquired by Sealink British Ferries, in 1987 this was increased to 42%.

Name	Year	NRT	GRT	LOA	BM	DFT	SPD	PAX
Lady of Mann (1)	1976	1,326	2,990	98.1	15.8	3.6	21	1,200
Mona's Queen (1)	1972	1,371	2,998	98.1	15.8	3.6	21	1,200
Peveril (2)	1971	684	1,976	106.3	16	5	14	12
Tynwald (3)	1967	1,309	3,630	112.5	17.4	3.7	19	1,200

Notes: (1) Can also carry light vans; (2) 1,685 dwt on charter from James Fisher & Sons PLC Heysham only; (3) all traffic.

ISLES OF SCILLY STEAMSHIP CO LTD

Hugh Street, St Mary's, Isles of Scilly TR21 0LJ
Tel: (0720) 22357

Although steamships were in use between Cornwall and Scilly from 1858, competition, bad weather, ill luck and poor organisation left the islands without a regular reliable steamer for considerable periods. Since the present company was founded in 1919, whose first owned ship appeared two years later, services have been maintained on a regular basis,

war years excepted. Two ships, each named in turn, *Scillonian*, have been remarkable for their longevity. The first lasted from 1926 to 1956, the second from 1955 to 1977, after which she traded elsewhere. The present mail/cargo/passenger ship retains the traditional lift-on, lift-off profile of former vessels engaged in the Penzance-Scilly services.

Name	Year	NRT	GRT	LOA	BM	DFT	SPD	PAX
Gugh (1)	1944	11.1	24	16.5	3.9	1.8	9	48
Scillonian III	1977	262	1,255	67.7	11.9	2.9	15.5	600

Notes: (1) Inter-island ferryboat; wooden hull.

JEBSENS SHIP MANAGEMENT LTD

Jebsen House, 53/55 High Street, Ruislip, Middlesex HA4 7AZ
Tel: (0895-) 676 341 *Telex:* 8950487

The Jebsen Group was founded in Norway in 1929, and since then has specialised in the carriage of dry bulk cargoes such as grain and coal, and also

in the handling of forest products, especially newsprint and woodpulp. British registered ships are managed from the London office.

Name	Year	NRT	GRT	DWT	LOA	BM	DFT	SPD
Binsnes (2)	1981	11,411	16,421	26,354	175.1	25.5	10	14.5
Bolnes (2)	1981	11,411	16,421	26,354	175.1	25.5	10	14.5
Lakenes (2)	1984	13,683	26,257	45,090	185.8	30.4	11.3	14
Rocknes	1975	2,296.6	3,644.6	5,790	102.3	15.6	6.9	14
Rollnes	1976	2,296.6	3,644.6	5,790	102.3	15.6	6.9	14
Telnes (1)	1982	4,281	6,792	10,110	117.9	20.5	8.5	14

Notes: (1) Fitted with own conveyor belt, self unloading, capable of handling 1,800 tonnes per hour; (2) are geared.

JOHN KELLY LTD

2 High Street, Belfast BT1 2BH
Tel: (0232) 243891 *Telex:* 74644

Originally coal importers and merchants from 1840, Kelly's bought their first ship, a brigantine, in 1861. Steamships entered the fleet as late as 1890, while the last sailing ship, the barquentine *Gartsherrie*, survived until 1901. Jointly owned in equal halves by Wm Cory & Son Ltd, and Powell Duffryn Ltd, since 1948, when family connections with the firm ended.

The present fleet of motor colliers trades mainly in the Irish Sea, but can be seen further afield on occasion.

Top:
Jebsens *Bolnes*. Courtesy: Fotoflite

Above:
J. P. Knight *Kenley*. Courtesy: M. J. Gaston

Below:
Lapthorn *Hoo Swan*. Courtesy: Fotoflite

Name	Year	NRT	GRT	DWT	LOA	BM	DFT	SPD
Ballygarvey	1982	915	1,599	2,535	77.9	13.3	5	12
Ballygrainey	1983	915	1,599	2,535	77.9	13.3	5	12
Ballykelly	1975	1,138	1,599	3,010	84.4	14.2	5.2	12
Ballykern	1976	1,185	1,598	3,110	84.4	14.2	5.2	12

J. P. KNIGHT LTD

348 High Street, Rochester, Kent ME1 1DH
Tel: (0634) 42408 *Telex:* 965016

Founded in 1892, Knight specialises in towage in the Thames Estuary and the River Medway. Several ocean-going pontoon barges and ancillary craft are owned and operated by associate company J. P. Knight (Offshore) Ltd. The company controls Caledonian Towage & Marine Services Ltd, and is associated with The Orkney Towage Co Ltd of Kirkwall.

Name	Year	GRT	LOA	BM	DFT	BP	SPD
Katra	1961	38	18.7	5.5	2.4	7.5	10
Kemsing	1960	135	28.1	7.5	3.3	16	11
Kenley (1, 2)	1985	290	36.3	10	3	45	13
Kennet	1965	278	34.5	9.1	4.6	30	12
Kent (3)	1948	121	24.7	7	3.2	7	10
Kestrel (1, 2)	1985	290	36.3	10	3	45	13
Knighton	1968	276	34.6	9.1	4.6	30	12

Caledonian Towage & Marine Services Ltd
107 High Street, Invergordon, IV18 0DN
(*Tel:* [0349] 852611 *Telex:* 75249)

Kendal	1973	282	32.4	9	4.5	35	12
Keston (1)	1970	299	34.7	9.1	3.3	40	12
Kinluce (1)	1966	451	39	9.5	4.3	25	13
Kinnaird (1)	1969	677	54	11.5	4.2	35	14
Kinross (1, 2)	1978	289	35	9.6	3.9	50	12

Notes: (1) Fire-fighting capability; (2) Z Peller propulsion; (3) withdrawn, leased to Museum of London. In addition the tugs *Kessock*, *Kinloch* and *Kintore* are operated from Kirkwall by the Orkney Towage Co Ltd.

R. LAPTHORN & CO LTD

Buttercrock Wharf, Hoo, Rochester, Kent ME3 9LQ
Tel: (0634) 250 369 *Telex:* 96350

Lapthorn, a family concern, was formed in 1951 and operated until 1963 exclusively in the barge business on the Thames and Medway. The company expanded into the home coasting trade in the latter year, and by 1972 the barging side had been completely abandoned. They now specialise in dry bulk cargoes with gearless tonnage.

Name	Year	NRT	GRT	DWT	LOA	BM	DFT	SPD
Hoocreek	1982	388	499	1,230	50	9.4	4.1	9
Hoocrest	1986	552	794	1,400	58.3	9.4	3.8	9
Hoo Dolphin	1986	552	794	1,400	58.3	9.4	3.9	9
Hoo Laurel	1984	552	794	1,400	58.3	9.4	3.9	9
Hoo Marlin	1986	552	794	1,400	58.3	9.4	3.9	9

Above:
London & Overseas Freighters *London Victory*.   *Courtesy: L&OF*

Below:
MacAndrew's *Pacheco* on charter to P&O Containers in 1987 as *Gerrans Bay*.
Courtesy: P&O

Name	Year	NRT	GRT	DWT	LOA	BM	DFT	SPD
Hoo Plover	1983	388	499	1,230	50	9.4	4.1	9
Hoopride	1984	552	794	1,400	58.3	9.4	3.9	9
Hoo Swan	1986	552	794	1,400	58.3	9.4	3.9	9
Hoo Tern	1985	552	794	1,400	58.3	9.4	3.9	9
Hoo Willow	1984	388	499	1,230	50	9.4	4.1	9

Note: *Betty Jean*, *Hoo Venture* and *Whitonia* are managed for John H. Whitaker (Holdings) Ltd (qv).

LONDON & OVERSEAS FREIGHTERS PLC
15 Fetter Lane, London EC4A 1EL
Tel: (01-) 583 5888   *Telex:* 22143

Founded by 'London Greeks' in 1948, London & Overseas Freighters at first operated both tankers and dry cargo ships on tramp trading worldwide. In recent years the company has concentrated purely on tanker business.

Name	Year	NRT	GRT	DWT	LOA	BM	DFT	SPD
London Spirit	1982	16,760	36,865	61,116	219	32	12.8	15.5
London Victory	1982	16,760	36,865	61,114	219	32	12.8	15.5

MacANDREWS & CO LTD
Baltic Exchange Buildings, 21 Bury Street, London EC3A 5AU
Tel: (01-) 283 1266   *Telex:* 892728

MacAndrews' traditional trading has been with Spain since 1770, when small sailing ships were chartered for north-bound fruit cargoes. In 1935 it became a wholly owned subsidiary of the United Baltic Corporation. The Iberian trade is still maintained with chartered foreign container ships, while MacAndrews' own geared multi-purpose container ships are usually on charter to others.

Name	Year	NRT	GRT	DWT	LOA	BM	DFT	SPD	TEU
Pacheco	1986	1,573	3,790	4,348	106.6	15.9	5.5	13	354
Palacio	1986	1,573	3,573	4,348	106.6	15.9	5.5	13	354

THE MAERSK CO LTD
Black Swan House, Kennet Wharf Lane, Upper Thames Street, London EC4V 3ET
Tel: (01-) 248 9666   *Telex:* 8812165

Founded in 1951, The Maersk Co Ltd is a subsidiary of Denmark's A. P. Moller Group, established in Copenhagen in 1904. The UK company specialises in the control and operation of non-liner vessels, notably product tankers, LPG carriers and off-shore oil support and supply vessels. The parent company operates one of the world's largest fleets of trans-oceanic container liner fleets, and is also interested in short-sea ro-ro cargo ferry companies, several of which serve UK ports. Names begin with the word 'Maersk' unless otherwise stated.

Name	Year	NRT	GRT	DWT	LOA	BM	DFT	SPD
M. Ascension (1)	1976	19,092	13,134	59,850	211.2	32.2	13.2	14

Top:
Maersk Co *Maersk Harrier*. *Courtesy: Fotoflite*

Above:
Maersk Co *Duke of Anglia*. *Courtesy: Fotoflite*

Below:
J. Marr (Fishing) *Armana*. *Courtesy: J. Marr Group*

Name	Year	NRT	GRT	DWT	LOA	BM	DFT	SPD
M. Cadet (2)	1972	3,404	9,327	11,835	127.9	20.5	9.2	12
M. Captain (2)	1977	3,393	9,445	11,743	128.5	20.5	9.2	12
M. Commander (2)	1976	3,393	9,445	11,630	128.5	20.5	9.2	12
M. Cutter (3)	1983	564.1	1,596.7	2,000	69.2	15.5	6.4	12
M. Defender (3)	1976	597.8	1,593.7	1,374	63.3	13.8	5.6	12
M. Gannet (1)	1977	11,947	18,029	32,389	171.4	25.7	11.4	14
M. Harrier (1)	1982	5,022	8,959	13,845	127.9	20	9.4	12
M. Highlander (4)	1984	3,622	12,072	26,000	79.2	63.4	19.8	—
M. Mariner (3)	1985	1,184	1,598	2,430	82	18.4	6.9	14
M. Nautilus (1)	1979	20,164	36,376	69,900	247.2	32.1	13.2	13
M. Navarin (1)	1977	20,164	36,376	69,900	247.2	32.1	13.2	13
M. Navigator (1)	1978	20,164	36,376	69,900	247.2	32.1	13.2	13
M. Neptune (1)	1978	20,164	36,376	69,900	247.2	32.1	13.2	13
M. Nestor (1)	1979	20,164	36,376	69,900	247.2	32.1	13.2	13
M. Nimrod (1)	1978	20,164	36,376	69,900	247.2	32.1	13.2	13
M. Ranger (3)	1980	579.9	1,592.6	2,000	67.1	15.5	6.5	12
M. Retreiver (3)	1979	579.9	1,592.6	2,000	67.1	15.5	6.5	12
M. Rider (3)	1982	579.9	1,592.6	2,000	67.1	15.5	6.5	12
M. Rover (3)	1982	579.9	1,592.6	2,000	67.1	15.5	6.5	12
M. Ruler (3)	1980	579.9	1,592.6	2,000	67.1	15.5	6.5	12
M. Runner (3)	1980	579.9	1,592.6	2,000	67.1	15.5	6.5	12
M. Worker (3)	1976	399.2	1,097.7	1,962	65.5	14	5	12
Duke of Anglia (5)	1977	1,167	2,632	3,526	122.9	21	4.8	15

Notes: (1) Product tanker; (2) LPG carrier; (3) North Sea supply/support vessel with up to 152 tonnes BP; (4) semi-submersible drilling rig fitted with heliport and deck cranes; (5) ro-ro cargo ship (12 drivers/passengers; 282 TEU).

J. MARR LTD GROUP

St Andrew's Dock, Hull HU3 4PN
Tel: (0482) 27873   *Telex:* 592211

Having its origins in 1897, the J. Marr Group is the only family fishing business of any size to survive, and this is only because the company has diversified into other activities, among which marine research of one type or another is predominant. The company pioneered the freezing of fish at sea in 1962, but now has no freezer vessels. The firm underwent re-structuring in March 1987, separate companies being set up to control different aspects of the group's business including the two referred to below. Fishing vessels are of the stern-trawling type, while the research and other ships are mostly converted trawlers.

J. Marr (Fishing) Ltd

Name	Reg	Year	NRT	GRT	DWT	LOA	BM	SPD
Armana	FD322	1976	156	387	737	33	8.5	11.5
Gavina	H24	1976	73	244	719	28	9.2	12
Glen Coe	A283	1973	113	299	—	28	8.4	12
Idena	FD325	1976	145	387	247	33	9.7	13
Jacinta	FD159	1972	184	599	—	48	9.8	12.8
Norina	FD324	1976	145	387	247	33	9.7	13
Omega B(1)	FD221	1973	173	408	183	39	8.4	14

Notes: (1) Part-owned with others. Two new deep-sea trawlers are on order for delivery in 1988. They will have stern trawling capability, a length of 38.5m and a beam of 9.7m.

J. Marr (Shipping) Ltd

Name	Year	NRT	GRT	LOA	BM	SPD	Type
Cumulus (1)	1963	357	1,974	65	12.8	12.8	Weathership
Falkland Desire*	1965	539	1,496	74.5	12.7	14.5	Fishery patrol
Falkland Right*	1968	315	928	69.3	12.1	14.5	Fishery patrol
Farnella	1972	560	1,207	70.2	12.7	16.5	Research
Lancella	1963	891	1,943	83.3	12.6	13	Fishery research
Northella	1974	463	1,238	70.2	12.7	16.5	Training ship
Northern Horizon	1966	567	1,493	75	12.4	15	Seismic survey
Pacific Horizon	1965	408	1,181	73	11	13	Seismic survey
Starella	1965	408	1,181	73	11	13	Research

Notes: *On charter to Falkland Islands Government; (1) owned by Ministry of Defence.

MERSEYSIDE PASSENGER TRANSPORT EXECUTIVE LTD

Victoria Place, Seacombe, Merseyside L44 6QY
Tel: (051-) 630 1030

Ferry services across the Mersey were legally originated by Royal Appointment (Edward III) in 1330. Somewhat later (in the 19th century), local borough councils became responsible for maintaining the various links, until 1969, when Merseyside Passenger Transport Authority took over control from Birkenhead and Wallasey councils. This responsibility passed to MPTE in 1974. Services, once prolific, are now maintained between Seacombe (Wallasey), Woodside (Birkenhead) and Liverpool Landing Stage. Vehicles have not been carried since 1941, after the first road tunnel, opened in 1934, had its predictable effect on ferry vehicle traffic.

Name	Year	NRT	GRT	LOA	BM	DFT	SP	PAX
Mountwood	1960	160	464	46.4	11.9	2.2	12	1,200
Overchurch (1)	1962	165	468	46.5	11.9	2.6	12	1,200
Royal Iris (2)	1951	622	1,234	47.9	14.7	2.6	12	1,200
Woodchurch	1960	159	464	46.4	11.9	2.2	12	1,200

Notes: (1) Acts as standby, and extra excursion vessel in summer; (2) usually engaged on public excursions and charter bookings.

MOBIL SHIPPING CO LTD

Mobil House, 54/60 Victoria Street, London SW1E 6QB
Tel: (01-) 828 9770   Telex: 8812411

The Mobil Shipping Co is responsible for the direct operation of all vessels owned by Mobil Oil Corporation and its subsidiary companies. Formed in 1954, Mobil in London controls a total fleet of about 28 oil product tankers, which trade worldwide with crude oil, petroleum products and chemicals. Most of this fleet (which is additional to other fleets controlled from the United States and Australia, for example) is registered elsewhere, mainly in Liberia, the British flag being carried by the following:

Name	Year	NRT	GRT	DWT	LOA	BM	DFT	SPD
Matco Avon (1)	1964	28,280	43,622	78,943	266.7	31.7	14.1	16
Matco Clyde (1)	1981	33,955	54,172	81,944	243.5	42.1	12.3	15

Above:
Mobil *Matco Clyde*. *Courtesy: Mobil Oil*

Below:
Natural Environment Research Council *Discovery*. *Courtesy: NERC*

Bottom:
Natural Environment Research Council *John Biscoe*. *Courtesy: NERC*

Name	Year	NRT	GRT	DWT	LOA	BM	DFT	SPD
Matco Thames (1)	1976	30,898	51,472	89,398	246.6	39.6	13.5	16
Mobil Lubchem (2)	1973	1,032	2,080	3,310	93.3	14	5.3	13

Notes: (1) Engaged in carrying crude oil from the Beryl Field in the North Sea to refineries and terminals in North-West Europe; (2) UK coastal and near-Continent waters.

NATURAL ENVIRONMENT RESEARCH COUNCIL

No 1 Dock, Barry, South Glamorgan CF6 6UZ
Tel: (0446) 737451

The Natural Environment Research Council, along with other research Councils, was established in 1965, to co-ordinate more closely, work in the field of oceanographic research. The prefix for the vessels is unique — RRS (Royal Research Ship). The ships spend varying periods at sea and give scientists high-quality facilities for research. The Council is partly funded by the Government and partly by contract with industry.

Name	Year	NRT	GRT	LOA	BM	DFT	SPD	PAX
Bransfield	1970	1,577	4,816	99.2	18.4	6.7	14	58
Challenger	1971	350	1,050	54.3	11.3	4.5	10	14
Charles Darwin	1983	580	1,936	69.4	14.4	4.9	11	18
Discovery	1962	668	2,321	79.6	14	5	10	20
Frederick Russell (1)	1974	153.9	546.7	43.5	9.4	4.1	11	8
John Biscoe (2)	1956	359	1,554	67.1	12.3	5	12	29

Notes: (1) Subject to withdrawal; (2) to be replaced by 1991.

NORTH BRITISH MARITIME GROUP LTD

Boston House, St Andrew's Dock, Hull HU3 4PR
Tel: (0482) 224181   *Telex:* 592511

The North British Maritime Group, formed in 1978, grew out of United Towing Ltd (itself founded in 1920), which was taken over by Hull shipping interests in 1960 and who later wanted a name which encompassed the more diverse interests with which the company was becoming involved. Apart from United Towing itself, other group companies include Boston Deep Sea Fisheries Ltd (renamed from St Andrew's Steam Fishing Co Ltd, in 1967 but which no longer owns any trawlers), Humber Tugs Ltd (formed in 1973 on the merger of J. H. Pigott & Sons Ltd, Grimsby), with the port tugs division of United Towing at Hull, and North British Shipping Ltd. The latter is involved in the operation of trans-Atlantic and other cargo services, usually with chartered ships. Other maritime members of the group include Cochrane Shipbuilders Ltd of Selby and Norbrit Wharfage Ltd of Briton Ferry, from where company cargo services usually operate. Boston Putford Offshore Safety Ltd is a joint Boston Deep Sea Fisheries/Putford Enterprises of Lowestoft venture, to provide safety services to the UK offshore industry, many of the vessels being converted trawlers. A controlling interest in the Group was acquired in 1987 by Howard Smith Ltd, a leading Australian publicly quoted company, to form a basis for their planned expansion in Europe.

Humber Tugs Ltd

Triton House, Alexander Road, Immingham Dock DN40 2LZ
(*Tel:* [0469] 77541   *Telex:* 52608)
The company specialises in estuary and dock towage within the River Humber area.

Name	Year	GRT	LOA	BM	DFT	BP	SPD
Keelman	1958	37	18.9	4.9	2.3	5.5	10
Lady Alma	1966	218	32.5	9	4	25	11.5
Lady Cecilia	1966	198	32.4	9	4	25	11.5
Lady Constance	1982	268	30.2	9.7	4.2	32	12.5
Lady Debbie	1978	348	34.5	10.5	5.3	50	11.5
Lady Elizabeth	1981	268	30.2	9.7	4.2	32	12.5
Lady Elsie	1970	263	32.8	9.5	5.1	40	12.5
Lady Laura	1967	114	25.3	7.3	3.2	16	10.5
Lady Marina	1967	114	25.3	7.3	3.2	16	10.5
Lady Moira	1977	348	34.5	10.5	5.3	50	11.5
Lady Sarah	1970	263	32.8	9.5	5.1	40	12.5
Lady Stephanie (1)	1984	268	30.2	9.7	4.6	32	12
Lady Susan (1)	1984	268	30.2	9.7	4.6	32	12
Lady Vera	1972	263	32.5	9.4	5.1	40	12.8
Riverman	1955	37	18.9	4.9	2.3	5.5	10
Seaman	1985	499	36	10.6	5.1	70	12.5

Notes: (1) Fitted with fire-fighting facilities.
Up to four new tugs are expected to be delivered during 1988, replacing some of the older ones listed above.

United Towing (Ocean Tugs) Ltd

Boston House, St Andrew's Dock, Hull HU3 4PR
(*Tel:* [0482] 224181   *Telex:* 597692)

United Towing has become recognised as one of Britain's leading deep-sea tug operators, attending long distance voyages with heavy lifts on pontoons, rigs and the like. Complex salvage work is also one of the company's activities.

Name	Year	GRT	LOA	BM	DFT	BP	SPD
Irishman	1978	686	42	11.6	4.9	72	13
Salvageman (1)	1980	1,598	69	15	6.1	170	17.5
Yorkshireman	1978	686	42	11.6	4.9	72	13

Note: (1) Equipped with fire-fighting facilities.

Boston Putford Offshore Safety Ltd

Columbus Buildings, Waveney Road, Lowestoft, Suffolk NR32 1BS
(*Tel:* [0502] 3366   *Telex:* 97332)

Formed by the Boston Deep-Sea Fisheries Ltd jointly with Putford Enterprises Ltd, the company markets the specialised safety services offered by the two promoters, Warbler Shipping and Breydon Marine. The fleet consists almost entirely of stand-by/rescue vessels, which operate all round the UK coast and are in a constant state of readiness in the event of an emergency arising on board oil rigs requiring the urgent disembarkation of personnel. Many of the vessels are converted stern trawlers, but new ones join the fleet from time to time.

In December 1987, Boston Deep Sea Fisheries' stand-by fleet was the subject of a management buy-out in the name of Britannia Marine of Lowestoft. The company name (BDSF) remains with North British, while the Boston Putford partnership continues in operation. The disposal of a number of stand-by vessels listed below can be expected over a period of time.

Above:
Humber Tugs *Seaman*. *Courtesy: North British Maritime*

Below:
United Towing *Salvageman*. *Courtesy: North British Maritime*

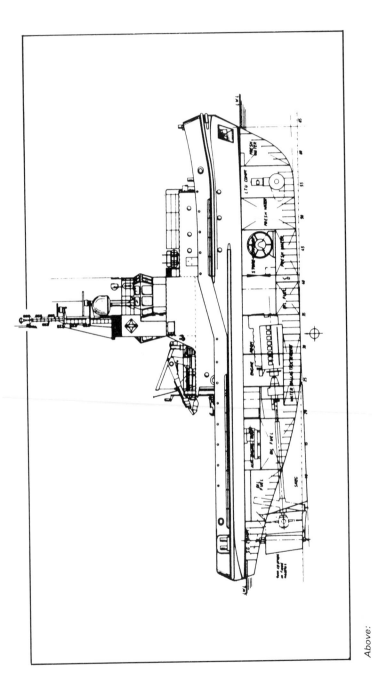

Above:
North British/United Towing deep sea harbour tug _Seaman_.
Courtesy: Cochrane Shipbuilders

Name	Year	GRT	DWT	LOA	BM	DFT	SPD	PAX
Blue Flame I	1976	1,450.5	1,900	62.3	14.5	4.8	11.5	20
Boston Sea Cobra	1978	211	139	26.3	7.9	3.2	10	150
Boston Sea Fury	1972	334	168	33.3	8.2	3.2	11	250
Boston Sea Gazelle	1978	211	115	26.2	8	2.8	10	150
Boston Sea Knight	1976	196	91	25.9	7.4	2.6	10	150
Boston Sea Stallion	1978	211	115	26.3	7.9	2.9	10	150
Boston Sea Vixen	1978	211	139	26.3	7.9	3.2	10	150
Dawn Gem	1958	183	—	32.4	7	2.9	10.5	150
Dawn Monarch	1961	237	—	35.2	7.6	3.2	11	150
Putford Dart	1972	312	168	33.3	8.2	3.2	11	250
Putford Guardian (1)	1967	499	805	51.1	11	3.8	11	Nil
Putford Harrier	1960	163	—	28.6	6.8	3	10	100
Putford Hawk	1953	115	—	26.8	6.2	3.4	9	100
Putford Merlin	1962	166	—	29.9	6.9	2.9	9	100
Putford Osprey	1960	230	—	33.1	7.2	3.2	11	150
Putford Scimitar	1959	135	—	28.1	6.8	2.7	10	100
Putford Skua	1967	664	—	52.4	11.4	4.2	10	250
Putford Tern (1)	1967	664	985	52.4	11.4	4.2	16	Nil

Note: (1) Anchor handling/support/tug (BP:20).

OCEAN FLEETS LTD

India Buildings, Liverpool L2 0RB
Tel: (051-) 236 9292   *Telex:* 629236

This company founded in 1967, acts as managers of deep-sea ships in the Ocean Transport & Trading Group, the latter coming into being in 1973 when the Ocean Steamship Co Ltd was renamed. Wholly owned shipping subsidiaries of O.T.T. PLC (changed from Limited in 1982) include the Wm Cory Group who are mainly involved in towage, Elder Dempster, Rea Towing and, the most recent acquisition, Palm Line in 1985. Partly owned companies are Forth Tugs and John Kelly Ltd, while the company is also involved in the Barber Blue Sea Line deep-sea trades, inaugurated in 1974 in partnership with Wilh Wilhelmsen and Swedish owners. Elder Dempster started West African operations in 1852.

Name	Year	NRT	GRT	DWT	LOA	BM	DFT	SPD	TEU
Apapa Palm (1)	1978	8,666	16,031	21,081	164.6	26.1	10.6	18	789
Barber Hector (2)	1984	15,871	27,990	43,986	262.1	32.3	11.7	21	2,455
Barber Perseus (2)	1979	11,999	21,747	32,434	228.5	32.3	10.8	21	1,778
Melampus	1977	8,666	16,031	21,618	164.7	26.1	10.6	18	789
Memnon (1)	1977	8,666	16,030	21,287	164.7	26.1	10.6	18	789
Menelaus (1)	1977	8,666	16,030	21,241	164.5	26.1	10	18	789
Nestor (3)	1977	51,244	78,915	78,400	274.4	42.1	12.9	19	Nil

Notes: (1) Combi-ships, usually engaged in Elder Dempster liner trades between UK and West African ports; (2) ro-ro/containerships mainly on trans-Pacific services; (3) LPG/LNG carrier, laid up.

ORKNEY ISLANDS SHIPPING CO LTD

4 Ayr Road, Kirkwall, Orkney KW15 1QX
Tel: (0856) 2044   *Telex:* 75193

This company, with its predecessors (it was reconstituted in 1961), has been operating inter-island services since 1868. It was taken over by Orkney Islands

Above:
Orkney Islands Co *Islander*.   *Author*

Below:
Princess Voyages *Pacific Princess*.   *Courtesy: P&O*

Bottom:
Princess Voyages *Royal Princess*.   *Courtesy: P&O*

Council in April 1987, the ships being transferred to the Council by the Scottish Office which had previously owned most of the fleet. The company continues to exist under its own name, and the services provided continue as before. The company operated the last coal-fired passenger-cargo ship in UK waters (*Earl Sigurd* 1931-1969).

Name	Year	NRT	GRT	LOA	BM	DFT	SPD	PAX	CARS
Clytus	1944	15.9	30.4	14.6	4.3	2	8	46	Nil
Eynhallow (1)	1987	28.4	79	21.3	7	1.6	9.5	95	8
Golden Marianna	1973	14	33	16.2	4.9	1.7	9.5	65	Nil
Hoy Head (1)	1973	76.4	147	22.6	7.8	2	9.5	84	10
Islander	1969	73.4	250	40.2	9.4	2.9	11.5	12	10
Lyrawa Bay (1)	1970	59	101.8	27.1	6.7	2.3	9.5	100	10
Orcadian	1962	285.6	619.2	50	11.4	2.9	12.5	281	10

Notes: (1) Passenger/Car Ferries (others are conventional). *Islander* is lo-lo cargo of 140 tonnes; *Orcadian*, is also lo-lo and can carry 100 tonnes.

P&O GROUP

79 Pall Mall, London SW1Y 5EJ
Tel: (01-) 930 4343   *Telex:* 885551

The Peninsular & Oriental Steam Navigation Co Ltd, celebrated its 150th anniversary in 1987. From small beginnings trading with Portugal, the company has grown to be the largest shipping company in the UK. Apart from the various companies, such as British India, which it had absorbed during its development, the most significant changes have taken place during the last two years.

P&O entered the UK short-sea ferry business for the first time in the late 1960s in the English Channel. Although these ventures were not really successful, this did not prevent the company from buying out European Ferries Ltd, and all its subsidiaries, early in 1987. With European Ferries, came the Townsend-Thoresen and Atlantic Steam Navigation Co ferry operations, the Monarch Steamship Co (technical owners of a number of ferries), and the ports of Cairnryan, Felixstowe and Larne. Townsend-Thoresen Ferries had its roots in the late 1920s, but in October 1987 the title was formally withdrawn from the records, all such ferry operations henceforth trading under the name of P&O European Ferries Ltd.

Meanwhile in 1986, P&O acquired complete control of Overseas Containers Ltd. OCL was formed in August 1965 by P&O, British and Commonwealth Shipping, Ocean Transport and Furness Withy, jointly, to provide container services to Australia. These started in 1969, followed by a similar service to Far Eastern ports in 1972.

Group ships are listed below according to their individual operating company. Of a total fleet of 73, a mere handful do not fly the British flag. Several tugs and off-shore service vessels operated by P&O Australia Ltd, fly the Australian flag, and are therefore not included.

All containerships listed are gearless. The sections which follow are divided into 'deep-sea' operations (first), followed by short-sea ferry activities.

Above:
P&O Containers *Kowloon Bay*. *Courtesy: Fotoflite*

Below:
P&O Containers *Providence Bay*. *Courtesy: P&O/Skyfotos*

DEEP-SEA OPERATIONS
'Canberra Cruises' and 'Princess Voyages'
77 New Oxford Street, London WC1A 1PP
(*Tel:* [01-] 831 1881   *Telex:* 885551

Name	Year	NRT	GRT	LOA	BM	DFT	SPD	PAX
Canberra (1)	1961	24,021	44,807	249.9	31.6	10	27	1,653
Island Princess	1972	11,165	19,907	168.7	24.6	7.5	21	624
Pacific Princess (1)	1971	11,703	20,636	168.7	24.6	7.7	21	624
Royal Princess	1984	19,646	44,348	230.9	32	8	22	1,192
Sea Princess	1966	13,842	27,670	201.2	26.6	8.7	21	778
Sun Princess	1972	8,885	17,370	163.3	24.8	8.6	25	703

Notes: In 1988, ships marked (1) will cruise mainly in European waters, the others in Caribbean waters and to Alaska.

P&O Containers Ltd
Beagle House, Braham Street, London E1 8EP
(*Tel:* [01-] 488 1313   *Telex:* 883947)

Name	Year	NRT	GRT	DWT	LOA	BM	DFT	SPD	TEU
Botany Bay (1)	1969	11,259	27,835	28,794	227.3	30.6	10.7	21	1,572
Cardigan Bay (2)	1972	17,046	56,822	47,442	289.6	32.3	13	23	2,700
Discovery Bay (1)	1969	11,259	27,823	29,288	227.3	30.6	10.7	21	1,536
Encounter Bay (1)	1969	11,259	27,835	28,787	227.3	30.6	10.7	21	1,572
Flinders Bay (1)	1969	14,663	26,756	29,262	227.3	30.6	10.7	21	1,572
Kowloon Bay (2)	1972	17,046	56,822	47,442	289.6	32.3	13	23	2,700
Liverpool Bay (2)	1972	17,046	56,822	47,442	289.6	32.3	13	23	2,700
Mairangi Bay (1)	1978	21,228	43,674	38,757	248.6	32.3	12	23	1,953
Moreton Bay (1)	1969	11,259	27,823	29,288	227.3	30.6	10.7	21	1,536
Osaka Bay (2)	1973	17,046	56,822	47,442	289.6	32.3	13	23	2,700
Providence Bay (2)	1983	17,480	33,267	34,477	216.1	32.3	11	17	1,940
Remuera Bay (1)	1973	12,544	41,814	32,713	251.3	32.1	11	24	1,813
Resolution Bay (1)	1977	21,228	43,674	38,757	248.6	32.3	12	23	1,953
Strathbrora	1978	7,507	15,503	21,207	178.4	26	9.4	18	1,266
Strathconan	1978	7,572	15,598	21,207	178.4	26	9.4	18	1,266
Tokyo Bay (2)	1972	17,046	56,822	47,442	289.6	32.3	13	23	2,700
Tolaga Bay (2)	1977	21,263	52,055	47,197	258.5	32.3	13	23	2,700
Tor Bay (2)	1982	17,480	33,267	34,477	216.1	32.3	11	23	1,940

Notes: Ships are usually engaged in the following trades from northern Europe to: (1) Australia and New Zealand; (2) Far East. New ship on order (3,600 teu) delivery mid-1989.

P&O Containers Ltd also operates three container ships on services between Australia/New Zealand and Far East ports, trading under the names Crusader Swire Container Service Ltd (the *Aotea*) and Australia Japan Container Line Ltd (the *Arafura* and the *Ariake*) in conjunction with John Swire & Sons Ltd (qv for details). Part-owned are the *Asian Jade* and *Asian Pearl* again with John Swire & Sons Ltd. In addition P&OCL charters container tonnage for its cross-trade service between East Africa, the Gulf and the Indian sub-continent. Also has interests in trans-Atlantic services.

P&O bulk shipping — world-wide tramping (P&O Ship Management Ltd)

Name	Year	NRT	GRT	DWT	LOA	BM	DFT	SPD
British Trident (1)	1974	108,853	133,035	275,333	388.6	53.7	20.7	15
Ormond (2)	1986	60,417	96,659	187,025	299.8	47.2	17.7	16
Quorn (2)	1983	25,957	36,209	63,800	225	32.3	13.1	15
Rutland (3)	1978	31,798	55,465	81,131	231	44	12.9	15
Snowdon (2)	1983	53,321	74,512	131,650	280	42.1	17	14

Notes: (1) Tanker on charter to BP; (2) bulk carriers; (3) tanker on charter to Howard Smith industries.

Above:
P&O Ferries *St Sunniva*.   *Courtesy: P&O*

Below:
North Sea Ferries *Norland*.   *Courtesy: P&O*

Bottom:
North Sea Ferries *Norsea*.   *Courtesy: P&O*

SHORT-SEA OPERATIONS
P&O Ferries Ltd
PO Box No 5, Jamieson Quay, Aberdeen AB9 8DL
(*Tel:* [0224] 589111   *Telex:* 73344 [passengers] 739156 [freight])

Specialises in the operation of ro-ro/passenger ferries between Scotland (Aberdeen and Scrabster) and the Orkney and Shetland Islands. Formerly known as the North of Scotland, Orkney and Shetland Shipping Co Ltd — whose origins can be traced back to 1790. They came into the P&O Group with Coast Lines in 1971 having been taken over by the latter in 1961.

Name	Year	NRT	GRT	LOA	BM	DFT	SPD	PAX
St Clair	1965	1,923	4,468	123.3	18.4	4.7	20	600
St Magnus	1970	411	1,206	96.8	16.4	4.2	14	12
St Ola	1974	575	1,344	70.1	14.7	4.1	16	400
St Sunniva	1972	1,441	4,211	104.4	18.9	4.6	15	407

North Sea Ferries Ltd
King George Dock, Hendon Road, Hull HU9 5QA
(*Tel:* [0482] 795141   *Telex:* 592349)

Jointly owned with Nedlloyd (Netherlands) this company runs ro-ro/passenger ferries between Hull and Rotterdam and Zeebrugge. Formed in 1964 specifically to operate ro-ro tonnage on the Hull-Rotterdam run the company was originally jointly owned by six companies. After 1971 two P&O Group companies (General Steam Navigation Co and Tyne Tees Shipping) combined to give the parent company a 45% share. This has now become 50%. North Sea Ferries also operates a ro-ro service between Ipswich and Rotterdam, inaugurated in 1978.

Name	Year	NRT	GRT	LOA	BM	DFT	SPD	PAX
Norland	1974	15,555	26,290	173.3	25.2	6	19	881
Norsea	1987	9,300	31,785	169.8	25.1	6.2	18.5	1,250
Norsky (1)	1979	2,091	6,310	150	21.8	5.1	18	12

Note: (1) Owned by P&O subsidiary Poets Fleet Management Ltd.

P&O European Ferries Ltd
Channel House, Channel View Road, Dover, Kent CT17 9TJ
(*Tel:* [0304] 223833   *Telex:* 965104)

This company was officially 'launched' on 21 October 1987, as the successor to what had been the European Ferries/Townsend Thoresen organisation, following P&O's takeover on 19 January the same year. Services from Felixstowe, Dover, Portsmouth and Cairnryan continue as before, offering passenger accommodation and full ro-ro facilities for cars and freight.

Name	Year	NRT	GRT	LOA	BM	DFT	SPD	PAX
Baltic Ferry	1979	10,578	18,732	151	23.5	7.3	17	682
European Clearway	1976	1,070	3,335	117.9	20.3	5.8	18.5	117
European Endeavour	1978	1,029	3,367	117.9	20.3	5.8	18.5	119
European Trader	1975	1,070	3,335	117.9	20.3	5.8	18.5	117
Europic Ferry	1968	1,499	4,190	138.3	21.1	4.6	18	160
Ionic Ferry	1967	2,732	6,141	134.6	21.9	4.8	17	843
Nordic Ferry	1978	10,578	18,732	151	23.6	7.3	17	682
Pride of Bruges	1980	3,439	7,951	132.5	23.2	5.7	23.5	1,326
Pride of Calais	1987	11,399	26,433	169.6	28.3	6.1	22	2,290
Pride of Canterbury	1974	2,048	5,170	123.6	19.5	4.4	20.5	1,123
Pride of Dover	1987	11,399	26,433	169.6	28.3	6.1	22	2,290
Pride of Hythe	1970	1,977	5,044	117.8	19.4	4.4	21	1,125

Top:
P&O European Ferries *Pride of Canterbury*.   *Courtesy: John F. Hendy*

Above centre:
P&O European Ferries *Baltic Ferry*.   *Courtesy: P&O*

Above:
P&O European Ferries *Pride of Bruges* as *Pride of Free Enterprise*.
Courtesy: John F. Hendy

Top:
P&O European Ferries *Pride of Calais*. *Courtesy: P&O*

Above:
Poets Fleet Management *Buffalo*. *Courtesy: P&O*

Below:
Poets Fleet Management *Elk*. *Courtesy: P&O*

Name	Year	NRT	GRT	LOA	BM	DFT	SPD	PAX
Pride of Kent	1980	3,439	7,951	132.5	23.2	5.7	23.5	1,326
Pride of Sandwich	1972	5,941	12,503	139.4	22.4	5.3	19.5	1,035
Pride of Walmer	1973	5,941	12,503	139.4	22.4	5.3	19.5	1,035
Viking Valiant	1975	7,014	14,760	143.7	23.4	5.4	20.7	1,326
Viking Venturer	1975	7,014	14,760	143.7	23.4	5.4	20.7	1,316
Viking Viscount	1976	2,918	6,387	143.7	23.4	5.4	21	1,200
Viking Voyager	1976	2,918	6,387	143.7	23.4	5.4	21	1,200

Poets Fleet Management Ltd
Station House, Stamford New Road, Altrincham, Cheshire WA14 1ER
(Tel: [061-] 928 6333   Telex: 668273)

This company has the responsibility for a miscellany of commercial vehicle ro-ro ferries, serving on Irish Sea and North Sea routes under several different P&O operational names. Northern Ireland Trailers (Scotland) Ltd, runs the Ardrossan-Belfast service (1); Pandoro Ltd the Fleetwood-Larne and Liverpool-Dublin services (2); while the Middlesbrough-Gothenburg connection (3) is maintained by Ferrymasters Ltd. The company was formed in 1985.

Name	Year	NRT	GRT	LOA	BM	DFT	SPD	PAX
Belard (1)	1979	843	1,599	105.6	18.8	5	15.5	4
Bison (2)	1975	1,695	4,260	141.8	19.1	4.7	18.5	45
Buffalo (2) (4)	1975	1,171	3,484	125	19.1	5.7	18.5	12
Elk (3)	1977	2,473	6,182	163.6	22.9	7.3	18.5	12
Puma (2)	1975	1,759	4,377	141.8	19.4	5.8	18	45

Note: (4) Being lengthened, spring 1988.

THE PADDLE STEAMER PRESERVATION SOCIETY

Through separate companies, the PSPS controls the activities of three excursion vessels which are in service during the summer months (usually Easter to September/early October). Operations started on the Clyde in 1975 with ps Waverley. The Balmoral has been included since 1986.

Waverley Excursions Ltd
Waverley Terminal, Anderston Quay, Glasgow G3 8HA
(Tel: [041-] 221 8152)

While Balmoral is mostly occupied in the Bristol Channel, with short periods in North Wales and the Solent, Waverley's activities are more widespread including sailings on the Clyde, Western Isles, South Coast and Thames.

Name	Year	NRT	GRT	LOA	BM	DFT	SPD	PAX
Balmoral	1949	310	736	62	9.8	2	14	800
Waverley	1947	327	693	73	17.7	1.9	15	1,016

Kingswear Castle Excursions Ltd
Chatham Historic Dockyard, Chatham, Kent
(Tel: [0634] 827648)

Operations on the Thames and Medway started with this former River Dart paddle steamer (still coal-fired) in 1984.

Above:
Paddle Steamer Preservation Society *Waverley*.   *Author*

Below:
Paddle Steamer Preservation Society *Kingswear Castle*.   *Author*

Name	Year	NRT	GRT	LOA	BM	DFT	SPD	PAX
Kingswear Castle	1924	—	94	34.7	8.5	0.9	8	235

REA TOWING CO LTD

169 Corporation Road, Birkenhead, Merseyside L41 1HS
Tel: (051-) 647 6652   *Telex:* 627867

This company originated in 1879 as Rea Shipping Ltd in Liverpool, which ran a fleet of small bunkering colliers around the major ports of the UK. Tug-owning started in 1895, curiously in Southampton, the first Merseyside tug appearing four years later. In 1918 this company and associate Bristol-based Rea Transport & Coaling Co Ltd, were taken over by Wm Cory & Son Ltd — but allowed to retain their identity. Rea Towing Co Ltd, as such was formed in 1922 to control Cory's interests on Merseyside, but now technically no longer exists as a separate company.

Name	Year	GRT	LOA	BM	DFT	BP	SPD
Beechgarth	1964	207	31	8.6	3.8	19	11
Brackengarth (2)	1969	330	36.6	10	5.6	50	14
Cedargarth	1962	213	30.5	8.6	3.8	18	11
Hazelgarth	1959	230	32	8.7	4.6	24	12
Hollygarth (2)	1969	330	36.6	10	5.6	50	14
Maplegarth	1962	213	30.5	8.6	3.8	18	11
Oakgarth (1, 2, 3)	1984	452	36	9.8	4.2	50	13

Note: (1) Serving Cabinda, Angola, 1988; (2) fitted with fire-fighting equipment; (3) Z Peller propulsion.

RED FUNNEL GROUP

(Southampton, Isle of Wight and South of England Royal Mail Steam Packet PLC)
12 Bugle Street, Southampton SO9 4LJ
Tel: (0703) 333042   *Telex:* 47388

Established in 1861, the company has operated passenger services between Southampton and the Isle of Wight ever since. Harbour and estuary towage was started in 1885. An extensive, regular excursion trade was built up over the years, but was abandoned in 1968. The company was notable for operating the last true tug-tender in UK waters, the second *Calshot*, withdrawn in 1985 (she was also used for occasional charter excursions), and for introducing high speed vessels in 1969 to the Cowes service. Four Italian RHS 70 hydrofoils are now available for this service. All other passenger vessels have drive-through ro-ro capability for all types of vehicles.

Passenger/Vehicle ferries

Name	Year	NRT	GRT	LOA	BM	DFT	SPD	PAX	CARS
Cowes Castle	1965	385	912	67.4	12.8	2.3	14	850	30
Netley Castle	1974	567	1,183	73.8	15	2.5	14	925	80
Norris Castle	1968	252	922	67.4	12.8	2.1	14	850	30
Shearwater 3 (1)	1972	31		61.9	22.3	4.9	2.7	32	67	Nil
Shearwater 4 (1)	1973	31		61.9	22.3	4.9	2.7	32	67	Nil
Shearwater 5 (1)	1980	31		61.9	22.3	4.9	2.7	32	67	Nil
Shearwater 6 (1)	1982	31		61.9	22.3	4.9	2.7	32	67	Nil

Note: (1) Hydrofoil.

Above:
Red Funnel *Shearwater 4*.   *Courtesy: Red Funnel*

Below:
Red Funnel *Totland*.   *Courtesy: M. J. Gaston*

Tugs

Name	Year	GRT	LOA	BM	DFT	BP	SPD
Clausentuum (2)	1980	334	33.2	10.3	4.2	36	12
Gatcombe (2)	1970	269	32.6	9.4	4.3	35	14
Hamtun (3)	1985	250	25.2	9	4.6	35	11.5
Sir Bevois	1985	250	25.2	9	4.6	35	11.5
Totland (4)	1961	161	28.9	8.4	3.8	17	10
Vecta (2)	1970	269	32.6	9.4	4.9	35	14

Notes: (2) Equipped for fire-fighting duties; (3) Schottle propulsion; (4) Voith Schneider propulsion.

J. R. RIX & SONS LTD

Carmelite House, Posterngate, Hull HU1 2JS
Tel: (0482) 26345   *Telex:* 592256

Still a family business, Rix can trace its sea-going activities back to the middle of the 19th century. The present company was founded in 1947 and specialises in the carriage of dry bulk and general cargoes such as steel, scrap, grain and stone, on near Continental and coastal routes. All such operations are on a tramp basis with gearless ships.

Name	Year	NRT	GRT	DWT	LOA	BM	DFT	SPD
Jemrix	1965	465.6	843.1	1,516	71.2	9.8	4.1	10
Magrix (1)	1976	699	998	1,897	78.4	10.7	4.1	10.5
Robrix	1975	435	799	1,184	61.7	10.5	4	11
Salrix	1965	383	655	1,421	65.2	9.8	4.5	10
Timrix	1972	504	818	1,393	72.7	10.5	3.8	11

Notes: (1) Being lengthened winter 1987/88.
The company also owns three small tank barges for the carriage and distribution of petroleum products within the Humber estuary, mainly from Immingham.

ROPNER SHIPPING CO LTD

140 Coniscliffe Road, PO Box 18, Darlington DL3 7RP
Tel: (0325) 462811   *Telex:* 58531

An old established company, Ropner specialises in the carriage of dry bulk cargoes especially iron ore, worldwide. All ships are gearless.

Name	Year	NRT	GRT	DWT	LOA	BM	DFT	SPD
Appleby	1978	38,842	64,124	117,613	261.5	40.7	16.2	14
Iron Kestrel	1974	9,715	16,819	27,269	177.9	22.9	10.9	15.2
Iron Kirby	1974	9,715	16,806	27,299	177.9	22.9	10.7	15.2
Lackenby	1977	38,842	64,124	119,500	261.5	40.7	15.2	14
Salmonpool	1982	76,050	24,575	43,728	204.9	27.2	11.79	15.25

Right:
J. R. Rix *Timrix*.   *Courtesy: Fotoflite*

ROWBOTHAM TANKSHIPS LTD

Glen House, Stag Place, London SW1E 5AD
Tel: (01-) 828 3466   *Telex:* 8950147

A member of the American Marine Transport Lines Group, Rowbotham started life in 1879 when Christopher Rowbotham became part-owner and master of the ketch *Princess*. Over the years the company grew, and began to specialise in the carriage of oil products and chemicals. In 1982 Hull Gates Shipping Co Ltd was taken over, which explains the presence in the fleet of several ships with names ending in '-gate'. Trading is engaged mainly in Northern European, Scandinavian and Mediterranean waters, though occasionally ships will go much further afield.

Name	Year	NRT	GRT	DWT	LOA	BM	DFT	SPD
Astraman	1973	1,079	1,579	3,202	87.4	13.7	5.9	14
Bridgeman	1972	2,308	3,701	6,210	103.6	14.9	7	12
Cableman	1980	3,369	4,916	8,496	116.5	17.5	7.1	13
Eastgate	1979	1,114	1,599	3,415	93.2	13.4	5.3	12
Echoman	1982	2,507	3,579	6,125	104.3	16.7	6.8	14
Helmsman	1972	2,308	3,705	6,068	103.9	14.9	7	13
Humbergate	1969	811	1,579	2,721	84.4	13.1	4.9	12
Irishgate	1981	1,124	1,599	3,284	93.2	13.4	5.2	12
Northgate	1981	1,124	1,599	3,290	93.2	13.4	5.2	12
Oarsman	1980	961	1,550	2,547	76.2	12.4	4.9	11
Oilman	1982	592	997	1,563	65.6	11.3	4.1	12
Orionman	1975	2,194	3,623	6,176	103.7	14.9	7.1	13
Pointsman	1970	1,530	2,886	4,620	99.3	14.4	6.2	12
Polarisman	1973	1,079	1,597	3,202	84.74	13.7	5.5	14
Quarterman	1973	761	1,226	2,135	72.8	10.7	4.9	11
River Shannon	1970	953	1,567	2,932	83.5	12.9	5.2	12
Tankerman	1983	4,145	5,881	10,716	119.7	19.2	8.1	12
Westgate	1979	1,124	1,599	3,367	93.2	13.4	5.3	12
Wheelsman	1967	1,536	2,897	4,575	98.3	14.3	6.1	12

Note: One or two 10/12,000dwt products tankers are expected to join the fleet in due course.

ST HELENA SHIPPING CO LTD

The Shipyard, Porthleven, Helston, Cornwall TR13 9JA
Tel: (0326) 563434   *Telex:* 45654

Following withdrawal of the UK-South African passenger/mail services in 1977 by Union Castle and Safmarine, St Helena Shipping was set up to manage this new link between the UK and St Helena in particular. The service extends to Cape Town, and calls are also made at Tenerife and Ascension.

Name	Year	NRT	GRT	DWT	LOA	BM	DFT	SPD
Bosun Bird (1)	1961	200	490	565	50	8.2	3.3	8
St Helena (2)	1963	1,894	3,150	2,264	95.1	13.9	4.9	14.5

Notes: (1) Tanker, based on St Helena; (2) 76 pax ship to be replaced by new building 7,500grt; 125 passengers; 1,500 tonnes cargo; due to be delivered 1990.

Top:
Rowbotham *Bridgeman.*   Courtesy: Rowbotham

Above:
Rowbotham *Eastgate.*   Courtesy: Rowbotham

Below:
St Helena Shipping Co *St Helena.*   Courtesy: R. A. Wilson

CHRISTIAN SALVESEN (SHIPPING) LTD

50 East Fettes Avenue, Edinburgh EH4 1EQ
Tel: (031-) 552 7101 *Telex:* 72222

Ever since the company was established in 1905 it has been associated with the whaling industry. As this died out about 1945, Salvesen turned more and more towards the carriage of bulk cargoes on short-sea and coastal voyages. Coal has predominated. The company also manages a number of ships for the Central Electricity Generating Board (qv). Movements are now coastwise UK, usually feeding power stations on the River Thames.

Name	Year	NRT	GRT	DWT	LOA	BM	DFT	SPD
Barra Head	1980	2,619	4,691	7,162	110.5	17.5	7	13
Rora Head	1980	2,619	4,691	7,162	110.5	17.5	7	13
Sumburgh Head	1977	2,630	4,694	7,174	110	17.5	7	13

SEA CONTAINERS LTD

30 Cedar Avenue, PO Box HM 1179, Hamilton, Bermuda
Tel: (809) 295 2244 *Telex:* 3223
Administration Office: **Sea Containers Services Ltd**
20 Upper Ground, London SE1 9PF.
Tel: (01-) 928 6969 *Telex:* 8955803

This company has specific interests in ferry and port operations on the one hand (through Sealink British Ferries) and container leasing equipment on the other. The latter includes containers, chassis, cranes and ships, which are chartered out mainly to liner operators for varying periods of time. Sea Containers do not operate any kind of shipping services as such. All ships are geared and have ro-ro capability, except *Hustler Indus*, which has neither.

Name	Year	NRT	GRT	DWT	LOA	BM	DFT	SPD	TEU
Boxer Captain Cook	1979	2,025.1	5,654.3	8,945	133.5	25	6.5	17	576
Contender Argent	1981	3,802.7	11,445.3	17,993	173	3.04	8.2	18	1,308
Fenicia Express (1)	1979	1,358	5,843	9,002	133.5	25	6.5	17	576
Forum New Zealand	1979	3,875.1	6,265.7	6,945	124.9	20	7.5	17.5	351
Hustler Indus	1973	902.2	1,598.9	2,153	85.3	13.7	4.7	13	124
Levante Express (1)	1979	1,358	5,843	9,002	133.5	25	6.5	17	576
Strider Crystal	1977	2,264.8	3,498.2	6,423	119	18.9	7.5	17	529
Strider Juno	1979	3,875	6,265.7	6,943	125	20	7.4	17	351
Tackler Dosinia	1979	1,162	2,800.2	4,500	114.7	19.5	5	15	378

Note: (1) To be renamed and converted to reefer ships.

SEAFORTH MARITIME LTD

Seaforth Centre, Waterloo Quay, Aberdeen AB2 1BS
Tel: (0224) 573401 *Telex:* 73387

Seaforth Maritime was formed in Aberdeen in 1972, to establish a British fleet of supply vessels to support the North Sea oil industry. The company is a registered Ministry of Defence contractor, being involved in vessel operations, off-shore contracts and project management. Owners of the company are James Finlay (55%) and Taylor Woodrow (45%) since 1978. All ships are of the supply type, each having a name with the prefix 'Seaforth'.

Top:
Salvesen *Barra Head*.   *Courtesy: Fotoflite*

Above:
Sea Containers *Contender Argent*.   *Courtesy: Sea Containers*

Below:
Seaforth Maritime *Seaforth Clansman*.   *Courtesy: Fotoflite*

QUARTER DECK

Above:
Seaforth's *Seaforth Clansman*, a new super breed of offshore support/supply and standby vessel. *Courtesy: Cochrane Shipbuilders*

Name	Year	GRT	DWT	LOA	BM	DFT	SPD	BP
Baronet	1986	850	970	53.9	12	4.2	10	Nil
Centurion	1983	1,599	2,200	68	15.6	6.4	11	140
Clansman (1)	1977	1,977	3,350	78.9	13.7	5	11.5	100
Conqueror	1976	1,432	1,235	68.4	13.7	5	11	114
Crusader	1983	1,599	2,200	68	15.6	6.4	11	140
Earl	1986	850	970	53.9	12	4.2	10	Nil
Emperor	1982	1,599	2,902	67.2	16.8	5.5	10	Nil
Highlander	1976	1,376	1,263	67	13.7	5	11	114
Minara	1983	1,065	1,969	68	14.5	4.7	11	140
Monarch	1982	1,598	2,900	67.2	16.8	5.5	10	Nil
Sovereign	1982	1,154	1,540	62.5	13.1	5	10	Nil
Viscount	1982	1,154	1,540	62.5	13.1	5	10	Nil

Notes: (1) Fitted with oil-dispersant spray equipment, buoy-winch (5-tonne) and helicopter decking. Can also accommodate up to 24 divers and supervisors plus five passenger/supernumeraries.

SEALINK UK LTD (SEALINK BRITISH FERRIES)

Sea Containers House, 20 Upper Ground, London SE1 9PF
Tel: (01-) 928 6969   *Telex:* 8955803

This company has its roots in the UK cross-channel and estuary ferry services operated by separate railway companies until nationalisation in 1948, which brought them all under the control of the British Transport Commission (Railway Executive). Later the shipping services were separated from the railway operations, Sealink (UK) Ltd being formed in 1979, and Sealink Harbours Ltd in 1982. In July 1984 Sealink was privatised and acquired by Bermuda-based Sea Containers Ltd, which now owns a 42% share in the Isle of Man Steam Packet Co Ltd (1985) and Hoverspeed Ltd outright in 1986. Services operate to Ireland, France, Belgium and Holland, and local services are maintained to the Isle of Wight and on the Thames, 14 different routes in total. Cross-channel services run from all but one of Sealink's seven ports (Newhaven), the others being Stranraer, Heysham, Holyhead, Fishguard, Folkestone and Harwich. A new service was opened between Liverpool and Ireland in spring 1988.

Passenger/Vehicle Ferries (all carry cars and commercial vehicles)

Name	Year	NRT	GRT	LOA	BM	DFT	SPD	PAX
Caedmon*	1973	404	764	57.9	18.7	2.3	10.5	756
Cenred*	1973	404	761	57.9	15.7	2.3	10.5	756
Cenwulf*	1973	404	761	57.9	15.7	2.3	10.5	756
Darnia	1977	1,636	3,455	114.4	18.1	4.6	17.5	412
Earl Godwin	1966	1,869	3,999	112.5	17.4	3.7	19.5	1,200
Earl Granville	1973	2,016	4,478	108.7	17.6	4.8	19	740
Earl Harold	1971	1,442	3,910	112.5	17.4	3.7	19.5	1,200
Earl William	1964	1,836	3,764	99.5	17.7	4.4	18	600
Galloway Princess	1980	2,675	6,268	129.4	21.6	4.5	19	1,000
Hengist	1972	2,008	5,590	117.5	19.8	4.1	19.5	1,400
Horsa	1972	2,008	5,590	117.5	19.8	4.1	19.5	1,400
Orient Express (1)	1975	6,198.6	12,343.2	152.1	22	6	19	791
Our Lady Pamela (2)*	1986	138	312	29.5	11.8	2.2	30	470
Our Lady Patricia (2)*	1986	138	312	29.5	11.8	2.2	30	470
St Anselm	1980	3,659	7,405	129.6	21.6	5	19.5	1,400
St Brendan	1974	2,774	5,426	120.8	19.5	5.9	18	1,400
St Catherine*	1983	856.5	2,036	77.1	17.2	2.5	12	1,000
St Cecilia*	1987	908	2,983	77.1	17.2	2.5	12	1,000
St Christopher	1981	3,655	7,391	129.6	21.6	5	19.5	1,400

Top left:
Sealink *Galloway Princess*. *Courtesy: Sealink*

Centre left:
Sealink *Orient Express*. *Courtesy: Sealink*

Bottom left:
Sealink *Our Lady Patricia*. *Courtesy: Sealink/Fotoflite*

Below:
Sealink *St Nicholas*. *Courtesy: Sealink*

Bottom:
Sealink *Seafreight Highway*. *Courtesy: Sealink*

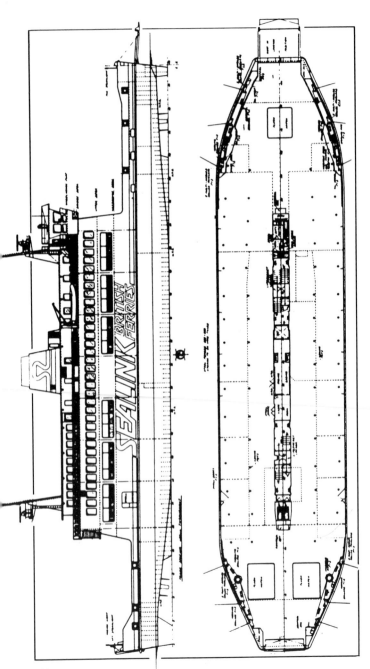

Above:
A multi-purpose ferry for the Sealink Isle of Wight service.
Courtesy: Cochrane Shipbuilders

Name	Year	NRT	GRT	LOA	BM	DFT	SPD	PAX
St Columba	1977	3,790	7,836	129.2	21.2	4.7	19.5	2,241
St David	1981	3,544	7,197	129.4	21.6	5	19.5	1,000
St Helen*	1983	908	2,983	77.1	17.2	2.5	12	1,000
St Nicholas (3)	1982	10,104	10,743	149	26	6.1	20	2,100
Southsea (4)*	1948	531	986	61	14.5	21.1	14	1,331

Notes: (1) Operates in Mediterranean, all others serve UK ports; (2) catamarans; no vehicle accommodation; (3) on charter from Stena of Sweden — option to purchase may be exercised; (4) passengers only; Isle of Wight service summer Saturdays; local cruises at other times. Available for charter.
*Engaged on Isle of Wight services.

Container Ships and Commercial Vehicle Ferries

Name	Year	NRT	GRT	DWT	LOA	BM	DFT	SPD	TEU
Brian Boroime (1)	1970	1,882	4,098	3,150	107.3	17.4	4.4	14.5	182
Cambridge Ferry (2)	1963	1,008	3,062	1,854	115.4	19.2	3.4	13.5	354
Rhodri Mawr (1)	1970	1,883	4,095	3,150	107	17.4	4.4	14.5	182
Seafreight Freeway (3)	1981	2,340	5,088	6,235	150.1	20.2	6.2	19	1,035
Seafreight Highway (3)	1981	2,340	5,088	6,235	150.1	20.2	6.2	19	1,035
Stena Sailer (4)	1975	735	2,353	2,495	119	16.3	4.2	17	435

Notes: (1) Containers only, gearless (Irish Sea); (2) rail/road ferry — to be withdrawn early 1988; (3) commercial vehicle ferries; 92 drivers/passengers (Dover-Zeebrugge/Dunkerque); (4) on charter from Stena, London; 12 drivers.

Miscellaneous Vessels

Name	Year	NRT	GRT	LOA	BM	DFT	SPD	PAX
Catherine (1)	1961	131	214	33.5	8.5	1.4	9	200
Edith (1)	1961	131	214	33.5	8.5	1.4	9	200
Meeching (2)	1960	—	152	29.3	7.7	3.4	12	Nil

Notes: (1) Engaged on Tilbury-Gravesend ferry service — passengers only (Catherine usually in reserve); (2) tug based at Newhaven (14 tonnes BP).

The Windermere Iron Steamboat Co Ltd
Ulverston, Cumbria LA12 8AS
(Tel: [05395] 31188)

This company is a subsidiary of Orient Express Hotels, an associate of Sealink British Ferries under the Sea Containers' banner. Operations on Lake Windermere under this title began in April 1985, when the business was taken over from Sealink (Windermere). The company is a direct descendant by takeover of the Furness Railway Co, which started Lake services in 1872, having itself taken over from previous operators.

Name	Year	NRT	GRT	LOA	BM	DFT	SPD	PAX
Swan	1938	166	251	41.5	7.6	1.5	11	616
Swift (1)	1900	138	203	45.7	6.4	1.5	13	724
Teal	1936	166	251	41.5	7.6	1.5	11	616
Tern	1891	64	120	42.7	5.5	1.4	12	450

Note: (1) Laid up, but could be returned to service in 1988.

Above:
Sealink *Edith*. *Author*

Below:
Windermere Iron Steamboat Co *Swan*. *Courtesy: Owners*

THE SHELL TRANSPORT & TRADING CO PLC

Shell Centre, London SE1 7PQ
Tel: (01-) 934 1234   *Telex:* 919651

Shell Transport & Trading has a 40% share in the parent company Royal Dutch/Shell Group, with Royal Dutch Petroleum Co holding the balance. The company specialises in the carriage of oils and oil products on a world-wide basis, in addition to delivering crude oil from North Sea terminals, such as Brent and Fulmar, to refineries in Europe and elsewhere. Shell Tankers (UK) Ltd, founded in 1912 and at the address above, operate the following mainly on deep-sea and North Sea trades.

Name	Year	NRT	GRT	DWT	LOA	BM	DFT	SPD
Drupa	1965	26,648	39,796	71,917	243.8	33.6	13.2	14
Ebalina	1980	12,030	18,654	31,374	170	26	11	14
Eburna	1979	12,030	18,654	31,374	170	26	11	14
Entalina	1978	11,975	18,092	30,990	169.4	26	10.9	14
Ervilia	1979	12,030	18,654	31,374	169.4	26	10.9	14
Erodona	1978	11,975	18,092	30,990	169.4	26	10.9	14
Etrema	1978	11,975	18,092	30,990	169.4	26	10.9	14
Eulima	1982	12,291	17,955	29,951	170.8	26	10.6	14
Eulota	1983	12,291	17,955	29,951	170.8	26	10.6	14
Euplecta	1980	12,030	18,654	31,374	170	26	11	14
Isocardia (1)	1982	11,979	39,932	47,989	210	31.4	10.4	17
Isomeria (1)	1982	11,979	39,932	47,594	210	31.4	10.4	17
Lampas	1975	122,871	153,687	31,996	351.4	55.4	22.4	14
Lanistes	1975	120,258	150,806	311,883	343.6	56.1	22.4	15
Leonia	1976	122,871	153,687	318,000	351.4	55.4	22.4	15
Lepeta	1976	122,871	153,687	317,996	351.4	55.4	22.4	15
Lima	1977	122,871	153,687	318,013	351.4	55.4	22.4	15
Naticina	1967	42,728	59,316	117,206	265.2	42.1	14.9	15
Northia	1971	42,629	68,286	133,560	280.1	41.2	16.7	15
Pomella	1967	10,699	15,842	25,250	175.2	22.8	10.1	15
Sentis	1985	25,376	50,272	79,900	234	40	12.2	14

Notes: (1) LPG carrier.

Shell (UK) Ltd

Shell Mex House, PO Box 148, Strand, London WC2R 0DX
(*Tel:* [01-] 438 3000   *Telex:* 22585)

Shell Craftsman	1968	762	1,528	2,257	75.9	12.5	4.7	11
Shell Director	1972	574	1,210	1,933	66.2	11.5	5	12
Shell Engineer	1966	525	1,177	1,522	65.5	11.4	4.3	11
Shell Explorer	1972	760	1,586	2,733	79	12.6	5.2	12
Shell Marketer	1981	1,027	1,599	3,027	79.3	13.2	5.5	12
Shell Seafarer	1981	1,027	1,599	3,027	79.3	13.2	5.5	12
Shell Supplier	1972	574	1,210	1,933	66.2	11.5	5	11
Shell Technician	1982	1,027	1,599	3,027	79.3	13.2	5.5	12
Shell Trader	1966	524	1,177	1,522	65.5	11.4	4.3	11

SHETLAND ISLANDS COUNCIL

Grantfield, Lerwick, Shetland ZE1 0NT
Tel: (095782) 259   *Telex:* 75218

Prior to the early 1970s, inter-island ferry services were provided only by small fishing-boat type vessels, with limited passenger accommodation. The oil boom led to the need to provide ro-ro services to improve communications, and the Coun-

Top:
Shell Transport _Eulota_. *Courtesy: Fotoflite*

Above:
Shell Transport _Leonia_. *Courtesy: Fotoflite*

Below:
Shetland Islands Council _Grima_. *Author*

cil took over full responsibility from about 1973. Five different ro-ro services are now provided between the main islands, though some lesser-used passenger-cargo routes are still served by small boats. Vehicle capacity varies between 10 and 15.

Name	Year	NRT	GRT	LOA	BM	DFT	SPD	PAX
Fivla	1985	69	230	29.9	9.6	2.5	11	95
Fylga	1974	76	147	25.3	7.9	2.1	8.5	93
Grima	1973	76	147	25.3	8.4	2.1	8.5	93
Hendra	1982	105	225	33.8	9.7	2.6	11	100
Kjella	1957	61	158	28.9	8	2.5	10.5	63
Thora	1975	76	147	25.3	7.9	2.1	8.5	93

Notes: Three new ships are expected to be delivered from the builders during the first half of 1988, replacing a similar number of older ones listed above.

SHETLAND TOWAGE LTD

Port Administration Building, Sella Ness, Shetland ZE29 QR
Tel: (080 624) 2708

Founded in 1978 to handle ships at Sullom Voe in the Shetlands, this company has been jointly owned throughout by Cory Ship Towage (later Cory Towage) 25%, Clyde Shipping Company 25% and Shetland Islands Council 50%.

Name	Year	GRT	LOA	BM	DFT	SPD	BP
Lyrie (1)	1978	392	38	10.5	4.4	11	54
Shalder (2)	1983	482	37.4	11.8	5.4	12	45
Stanechakker (1)	1978	392	38	10.5	4.4	11	54
Swaabie (1)	1978	392	38	10.5	4.4	11	54
Tirrick (2)	1983	482	37.4	11.8	5.4	12	45

Notes: (1) Fitted with fire-fighting equipment; (2) Voith Schneider propulsion.

STAR OFFSHORE SERVICES MARINE LTD

6 Albyn Terrace, Aberdeen AB1 1YD
Tel: (0224) 645 345   *Telex:* 73506

'SOS' was formed in 1974 for the purpose of providing specialised vessels to service North Sea oil platforms. Apart from *Star Hercules*, which can accommodate 42, the rest of the fleet can each carry 12 passengers. All ships' names as listed below are preceded by the word 'Star'.

Name	Year	NRT	GRT	DWT	LOA	BM	DFT	SPD
S. Altair	1985	654	1,704	2,270	68.2	15.5	5.2	11
S. Aries	1977	528	1,592	2,220	66.9	14.5	4.8	13
S. Capella	1983	827	1,599	2,036	68	15.5	5.2	11
S. Hercules	1980	635	1,598	2,300	82.2	17.3	4.5	12
S. Perseus	1979	153	493	396	43.6	9.5	3.2	10
S. Polaris	1983	426	1,420	1,900	64.6	13.8	6.2	12
S. Sirius	1985	467	1,558	2,000	65	14.5	6.4	12
S. Spica	1985	467	1,558	2,000	65	14.5	6.4	12
S. Vega	1983	827	1,599	2,036	68	15.5	5.2	11

STEPHENSON CLARKE SHIPPING LTD

Europe House, World Trade Centre, London E1 9AJ
Tel: (01-) 709 9188   *Telex:* 887141

Founded in 1730, the company's predecessors Clarke Brothers, traded on a world-wide basis with general cargo. More recently Stephenson Clarke began to concentrate on moving coal and other bulk dry cargoes both coastwise and mainly within Europe and the Mediterranean. Part of the Powell Duffryn Group. The *Ashington* made history in 1986 by being the first ship to have the Walker Wingsale fitted for trial purposes (see illustration). All ships are gearless.

Name	Year	NRT	GRT	DWT	LOA	BM	DFT	SPD
Aldrington	1978	2,228	4,334	6,570	103.6	16.1	7	14
Ashington	1979	2,228	4,334	6,570	103.6	16.1	7	14
Beeding	1971	1,114	1,595	3,221	87	12.7	5	12
Birling	1977	1,002	1,584	4,300	91.3	14.7	5.8	14
Dallington	1975	4,839	7,658	12,138	137.6	18.7	7.9	14
Donnington	1975	4,839	7,658	12,139	137.6	18.7	7.9	14
Durrington	1981	4,793	7,673	11,990	137.6	18.7	7.9	14
Emerald	1978	1,002	1,584	4,300	91.3	14.6	5.8	14
Gem	1969	1,194	1,599	2,967	90.8	13.4	5.2	12
Harting	1981	1,009	1,589	4,300	91.2	14.6	5.8	14
Malling	1970	992	1,596	2,880	86.9	13.2	5.3	12
Steyning	1983	1,009	1,589	4,300	91.3	14.6	5.8	14
Storrington	1982	4,793	7,673	11,990	137.6	18.7	7.9	13
Washington	1977	4,078	6,236	9,008	127	18.7	7.6	14

STIRLING SHIPPING CO LTD

16 Woodside Crescent, Glasgow G3 7UT
Tel: (041-) 332 9766   *Telex:* 77203

Founded in 1974 in the wake of the growing demand for North Sea and other area off-shore oil industry platform supply vessels, Stirling is jointly owned by Harrison's (Clyde) Ltd (the majority shareholder) and Scotts of Greenock (1911) Ltd. Two subsidiaries, as indicated below, are responsible for ancillary activities. All vessels have passenger accommodation.

Name	Year	NRT	GRT	LOA	BM	DFT	SPD	PAX
Stirling Albion	1982	402	1,340	59	14	6.1	13.8	12
Stirling Cormorant	1979	315	821.5	61.1	11.6	4	13	12
Stirling Dee	1985	560	1,403	64.6	14	5.3	12	12
Stirling Eagle	1975	299	699	55.3	11.6	3.9	12.5	12
Stirling Elf	1983	238	652	52	11	4.1	11	12
Stirling Esk	1986	572	1,399	65.1	14	5.3	12	12
Stirling Imp	1982	287	591	52	11	4.2	11	12
Stirling Merlin	1982	287	591	52	11	4.2	11	12
Stirling Osprey	1979	315	822	61	11.6	4	13	12
Stirling Puck	1982	286.8	591.5	52	11	4.2	11	12
Stirling Skua	1979	315	822	61	11.6	4	13	12
Stirling Snipe	1982	351	840	61.8	11.6	4	13	12
Stirling Sprite	1983	286.8	591.5	52	11	4.2	11	12
Stirling Teal	1982	351	840	61.8	11.6	4	13	12
Stirling Tern	1980	310.4	827	61	11.6	4.1	13	12

Seadive Ltd: Diving Support Vessels

Sea Mussel	1974	257	856	55.3	11.6	3.9	12.5	41
Sea Oyster	1976	267	856	55.3	11.6	3.9	12.5	41

Haven Shipping: Standby Safety Vessel

Stonehaven	1974	377.9	783.8	55.3	11.6	3.9	12.5	12

STRATHCLYDE REGIONAL COUNCIL

Department of Roads, Strathclyde House, 20 India Street, Glasgow G2 4PF
Tel: (041-) 204 2900   *Ext:* 2457

As successor to other owners and Clyde Port Authority in 1975, SRC operates a number of short ferry services in Western Scotland, between Renfrew and Yoker (on the Clyde at Glasgow), Port Appin and Lismore, Seil and Luing, and at Easdale.

Name	Year	NRT	GRT	LOA	BM	SPD	PAX
Belnahua (2)	1972	—	35	15.2	—	8	40
Highlander	1968	(timber launch)		8.4	—	—	23
Oronsay	1970	—	—	7.9	—	—	21
Renfrew Rose (2)	1984	34.4	65	17.1	5.5	9.3	50
Torsay (1)	1952	(timber launch)		7.6	—	10	15
Yoker Swan (2)	1984	34.5	65	17.1	5.5	9.3	50
'no name' (GRP launch for Easdale service)					—	10	10

Notes: (1) To be replaced; type and specification of replacement vessel under review;
(2) indicates ro-ro capability (*Renfrew Rose* and *Yoker Swan* have dedicated space for one ambulance).

SUFFOLK MARINE LTD

Waveney Chambers, Waveney Road, Lowestoft, Suffolk NR32 1BP
Tel: (0502) 2301   *Telex:* 97319

This company has been involved in the off-shore oil and gas industry since the early 1960s, providing survey, safety standby and supply vessels, as part of the Small & Co (Shipping) Ltd Group, originally established in 1826. Since 1974 the fleet has been completely renewed, so that the company is now in a good position to cope with virtually any eventuality. All vessels' names have the 'Suffolk' prefix.

Name	Year	NRT	GRT	LOA	BM	DFT	SPD	BP
S. Champion (1)	1980	108	350	33.2	9.2	4	11.5	15
S. Conquest (1, 2)	1974	134	433	40	8.8	4.4	14	25
S. Harvester (1, 3)	1974	129	433	40	8.8	4.4	14	25
S. Mariner (2, 3)	1986	647	1,432	60.1	14.1	5.7	12.5	Nil
S. Monarch (1, 3)	1974	129	433	40	8.8	4.4	14	25
S. Prince (4)	1982	402	985	60	12.8	4.5	14	50
S. Princess (4)	1982	401	985	60	12.8	4.5	14	50
S. Warrior (1, 3)	1974	134	433	40	8.8	4.4	14	25

Notes: (1) Rescue vessel; (2) supply vessel; (3) fire-fighting capability; (4) anchor handling/tug/supply vessel combined.

Above:
Strathclyde Regional Council *Belnahua*.   *Author*

Below:
Suffolk Marine *Suffolk Princess*.   *Courtesy: Suffolk Marine*

Above:
John Swire *Coral Princess*. *Courtesy: John Swire*

Below:
John Swire *Papuan Chief*. *Courtesy: John Swire*

JOHN SWIRE & SONS LTD

Regis House, 43/46 King William Street, London EC4R 9BE
Tel: (01-) 623 3030 *Telex:* 888800

Established in 1816 in Liverpool, the company's founders were particularly associated with trading in the Far East, notably China. In 1870, the headquarters were moved to London, by which time the agency business was growing, with extensive trading interests in China, Hong Kong, Japan and the Philippines. Ship owning started at about the same time and many subsidiary companies were later set up including the China Navigation Company. The Australian market also became important. The company is still a family concern, the present chairman being the fifth generation of Swires to serve the company. Some of the ships listed below are engaged in the Far East international container trades, mostly in conjunction with P&O Containers, others are bulk carriers and tankers as indicated. Chartering-out to other operators is commonplace.

Name	Year	NRT	GRT	DWT	LOA	BM	DFT	SPD	TEU
Aotea (1a)	1970	9,625	25,407	23,891	213	30	10.7	23	1,138
Arafura (1a)	1970	14,126	25,247	23,016	211.5	30.1	10.5	17	1,148
Ariake (1a)	1976	24,233	37,487	34,345	237.8	32.3	11.5	26	1,784
Asian Jade (1a)	1978	10,823	21,121	24,383	186	27.7	10.6	15	1,176
Asian Pearl (1a)	1978	10,824	21,122	24,354	186	27.6	10.6	20	1,176
Coral Chief (1b)	1977	3,134	6,373	7,078	117	20	7.1	15	320
Coral Princess (2)	1962	4,683	9,765	—	132	18.6	5.6	16.5	Nil
Eriskay (3)	1975	92,966	115,966	229,936	330	68	19.9	16.5	Nil
Hunan (4)	1981	16,279	23,410	40,507	182	29	11.4	15	—
Hupeh (4)	1984	14,650	26,239	45,260	183	31	11.9	14.6	—
Kweilin (1b)	1981	8,543	16,289	21,889	178.5	23	10.1	15.7	875
Papuan Chief (1b)	1977	4,098	7,354	8,710	117	20	7	15	392
Polynesia (1c)	1979	4,837	8,083	12,276	137.5	22.4	8	16	
Stolt Sceptre (3)	1971	9,180	15,401	23,840	169.7	24.8	9.7	15.8	
Stolt Stane (3)	1971	9,180	15,401	23,840	169.7	24.8	9.7	15.8	
Stolt Templar (3)	1971	9,180	15,401	23,840	169.7	24.8	9.7	15.8	Nil

Notes: (1a) Gearless part-owned containerships; (1b) geared container ships; (1c) geared part-owned container ship; (2) cruise liner (520 passengers); (3) oil tankers; (4) geared bulk carriers.

TEES TOWING CO LTD

Tees Wharf, Dockside Road, Middlesbrough, Cleveland TS3 6AB
Tel: (0642) 247273

This company was formed by the merger of The Robinson Tug Co Ltd with the Tees Co Ltd, in 1920, and in 1980 celebrated the centenary of the birth of the predecessors' founder W. H. Crossthwaite. It is still a family concern, operating tugs on the Tees and near continental areas.

Name	Year	GRT	LOA	BM	DFT	BP	SPD
Coatham Cross (1)	1981	186	27.9	8.8	5	35	11.5
Eston Cross (2)	1985	189	27.9	8.8	5	43	11.7
Greatham Cross (1)	1975	193	27.9	8.8	5	31.5	10
Norton Cross (2)	1984	189	27.9	8.8	5	43.8	11.6
Ralph Cross	1974	244	32.2	8.3	5	42	12.3
Skelton Cross (1)	1975	193	27.9	8.8	5	31.5	10
Yarm Cross (1)	1979	189	27.9	8.8	5	35.6	11.6

Notes: (1) Twin Schottle units; (2) twin Aquamaster units.

Top:
Tees Towing *Eston Cross*. *Courtesy: Tees Towing*

Above:
Texaco *Texaco Westminster*. *Courtesy: Texaco/Skyfotos*

Below:
Trinity House *Mermaid*. *Courtesy: Trinity House*

TEXACO LTD

1 Knightsbridge Green, London SW1X 7QJ
Tel: (01-) 584 5000   *Telex:* 8956681

Founded in Texas in 1902, the company opened its London office in 1916, thereby celebrating its 70th anniversary in 1986. Over the years the company absorbed other well known names, including Regent (1967) and the UK interests of Chevron and Getty Oil in 1984. North Sea oil interests were first held in the wholly owned Tartan platform which started operations in 1981. A large fleet of tankers is maintained, of various nationalities. The two listed below are engaged mostly in North Sea/near Continent crude oil movements.

Name	Year	NRT	GRT	DWT	LOA	BM	DFT	SPD
Texaco Westminster	1981	22,574	49,809	81,282	246.9	39.9	12.2	14
Texaco Windsor	1980	22,574	49,809	79,997	242.3	39.9	12.7	15

TORBAY SEAWAYS LTD

5 Beacon Quay, Torquay, Devon
Tel: (0803) 214397   *Telex:* 42500

This is a family business which first became involved in ship owning in 1981. The company concentrates on services to the Channel Islands from Torquay (1) and Poole (2), and general cargo tramping in the English Channel.

Name	Year	NRT	GRT	DWT	LOA	BM	DFT	SPD
Devoniun (1)	1964	709	1,420	—	71.6	14.1	2.7	14.5
Star Libra	1958	259	429	720	52.3	8.9	3.5	9
L. Taurus (2)	1971	552	982	1,542	80.7	12.9	4.2	14

Notes: (1) 300 pax; 50 cars/light vans (sideloading); (2) 180 cars.

TRINITY HOUSE LIGHTHOUSE SERVICE

Trinity House, Tower Hill, London EC3N 4DH
Tel: (01-) 480 6601   *Telex:* 884300

Originally founded in 1514 by Henry VIII, Trinity House was associated particularly with pilotage and lighthouse/lights maintenance. It is a statutory body, whose pilotage duties are to be transferred to port authorities in accordance with the terms of the Pilotage Act (1987). In the meantime, the Lighthouse service is in the process of discontinuing or altering characteristics of its 17 lights, 118 buoys, and totally discontinuing or transferring to port authorities its 24 lighthouses.

Name	Year	NRT	GRT	LOA	BM	DFT	SPD
Patricia	1982	791	2,541	86.3	13.8	4.4	12
Mermaid	1987	846	2,820	80.4	14.5	4.8	12
Stella (1)	1961	455.1	1,425	67.4	11.5	4	12
Winston Churchill (1)	1963	470	1,451	67.7	11.5	4	12

Notes: (1) To be sold 1988/89.
Four small back-up launches, *Farne*, *Burhon* and *St Tudwal* plus one new one, are also employed in light attendance and wreck-marking duties.

TURNBULL SCOTT SHIPPING CO LTD

Abbey House, Farnborough Road, Farnborough, Hants GU14 7ND
Tel: (0252) 548541   *Telex:* 858461

Although registered in London in 1911, the company has its origins, through family connections, in Whitby in 1840. At one time or another Turnbull Scott has been involved in most shipping activities, but recently has concentrated on the movement of bulk liquids on a worldwide basis.

Name	Year	NRT	GRT	DWT	LOA	BM	DFT	SPD
Irishgate (1)	1981	1,124	1,599	3,290	93.5	13.4	5.2	12
Stainless Spray (2)	1985	2,348	6,471	10,400	118.4	19.5	8.1	12

Notes: (1) Products tanker, operated by Rowbotham (qv); (2) chemical tanker (stainless steel tanker).

TYNE & WEAR TUGS LTD

Lawson-Batey Tugs Ltd
27 Market Place, South Shields NE33 1JF
Tel: (091-) 455 3361   *Telex:* 53730

Formed early in 1986, on the merger of Tyne Tugs Ltd and Wear Tugs Ltd, the company operates vessels owned by the parent company, Lawson-Batey Tugs Ltd. This latter company originated in 1895 and became a wholly owned subsidiary of Clyde Shipping Co in 1983. Operations cover local Tyne & Wear and the near continent.

Name	Year	GRT	LOA	BM	DFT	BP	SPD
Cragsider	1976	266	32.2	9.1	4.9	46	14
Holmsider	1984	150	28	7.4	3.8	18	11.5
Ironsider	1967	156	30.4	8	3.8	18.5	11.5
Northsider	1967	156	30.4	8	3.8	18.5	11.5
Seasider (1)	1985	164	28	7.4	3.5	18	11.5
Tynesider	1981	150	28	7.4	3.5	17	11.5
Wearsider	1980	150	28	7.4	3.5	17	11.5

Note: (1) Owned by Clyde Shipping Co Ltd

UNITED BALTIC CORPORATION LTD

Baltic Exchange Buildings, 21 Bury Street, London EC3A 5AU
Tel: (01-) 283 1266   *Telex:* 892728

Now a member of the Andrew Weir group of companies, the United Baltic Corporation was originally jointly set up by Weir and Denmark's East Asiatic Co in 1919 to trade in the Baltic. Shipowning started in 1920, catering for passengers and cargo. Services now operate to Finland, with a 50% interest in Finanglia (ro-ro) and Leningrad (container), UBC being the only UK line to offer regular services to the USSR. Up to 12 pax carried on Finnish service.

Name	Year	NRT	GRT	DWT	LOA	BM	DFT	SPD
Baltic Eagle (1)	1979	2,896.6	6,376.5	9,450	137.5	23.7	8	18
Baltic Osprey (2)	1972	464.6	998.4	2,167	88.3	13.7	4.4	14
Baltic Progress (3)	1974	1,511.6	4,665.4	5,615	132.2	22.3	6.7	18
Lady Franklin (4)	1970	1,018.4	2,124.8	3,627	103.4	15.6	5.9	15

Above:
Tyne & Wear *Holmsider*. *Courtesy: M. J. Gaston*

Below:
United Baltic *Baltic Eagle*. *Courtesy: United Baltic/Skyfotos*

Notes: (1) Ro-ro, 354 TEU; (2) container, 148 TEU (to be replaced on Leningrad service by new-building, due date late 1988, with about 350 TEU capacity); (3) ro-ro 290 TEU; (4) sto-ro, 107 TEU.
A new ro-ro ship owned by UBC for the Finanglia operation is expected to enter service at the end of the 1988/early 89, which may replace *Baltic Progress*.

WESTERN FERRIES (CLYDE) LTD

16 Woodside Crescent, Glasgow G3 7UT
Tel: (041-) 332 9766   *Telex:* 77203

A ro-ro operator throughout, the company started operations in 1968 between Kintyre and Islay, southwest Scotland. This service has now been terminated, but others are maintained across the Upper Clyde, and between Islay and Jura. All types of wheeled traffic are carried as well as passengers. Associated with Harrisons (Clyde) Ltd.

Name	Year	NRT	GRT	LOA	BM	DFT	SPD	PAX	CARS
Sound of Gigha (1)	1966	40.8	65.4	25.1	5.8	1	7.5	28	8
Sound of Sanda	1938	138.9	274.8	45	7.9	1.7	9	161	20
Sound of Scarba	1960	66.8	175.1	36.1	8	2	10	200	22
Sound of Seil	1959	146.4	362.7	45.2	12.6	1.6	10	400	26
Sound of Shuna	1962	84.8	243.8	41.9	9	1.1	10	200	24

Note: (1) Operated by sister company Western Ferries (Argyll) Ltd.

WESTMINSTER DREDGING CO LTD

Duke's Keep, Marsh Lane, Southampton SO9 7AG
Tel: (0703) 38611   *Telex:* 47516

Associated with dredging operators in the Netherlands, the UK company was formed in 1963 and is active in most home waters, particularly where extensive work is required. All vessels are hopper dredgers, and the company also owns and operates a number of hopper barges.

Name	Year	NRT	GRT	DWT	LOA	BM	DFT	SPD
W. D. Gateway	1969	4,496	8,168	6,100	129	19.5	8.7	16
W. D. Hilbre	1966	606	1,225	—	71.2	11.8	4.2	11
W. D. Medway	1976	944	1,962	4,376	75	15.1	5.2	11.8
W. D. Seaway	1963	3,102	4,712	5,829	110	18.5	6.5	12
W. D. Severn	1974	401	1,337	2,060	69	13	4.2	11
W. D. Tideway	1966	2,074	4,030	4,191	101	16.7	6	12

JOHN H. WHITAKER (HOLDINGS) LTD

Crown Dry Dock, Tower Street, Hull HU9 1TY
Tel: (0482) 20444   *Telex:* 597632

Still a family business, Whitakers was originally founded in 1880, becoming a limited company in 1910. In earlier days, the group concentrated on the carriage of dry cargoes, tankers being introduced in the mid-1920s. Gradually the bulk liquid business became more important, particularly in oils and petrol, and the dry cargo activities virtually ceased in the mid-1960s. The Humber assets of John

Below:
Westminster Dredging _W. D. Medway_. *Courtesy: Fotoflite*

Harker Ltd, and Cory Tank Craft Ltd, were acquired in 1976 and integrated in the Whitaker fleet. Tanker operations are carried on mainly on the Humber and canals of south and west Yorkshire, the Tyne-Tees area and on the Mersey, Manchester Ship Canal and Weaver Navigation. The company is also involved extensively in storage, bunkering, and small ship and barge building and repair. (The Yorkshire Dry Dock Co Ltd was acquired in 1917.)

John H. Whitaker (Tankers) Ltd — Humber Area

Name	Year	NRT	GRT	DWT	LOA	BM	DFT	SPD
Battlestone	1968	199.6	293.2	500	55.4	5.6	2.4	9
Blackbird	1959	75.1	141	250	43.3	5.3	2.4	8
Brocodale	1961	173.2	97.2	300	43.6	5.3	2.4	8
Cotterdale	1960	80	158	275	43.3	5.3	2.4	8
David W	1956	136.1	213.1	330	45.9	5.5	2.4	8
Dunlin	1960	109.1	174.6	270	44.9	5.4	2.3	8
Fossdale H	1967	199.6	293.2	430	55.4	5.6	2.4	9
Fusedale H	1968	199.6	293.2	430	55.4	5.6	2.4	9
Humber Dawn	1977	125.9	291.1	400	45.7	7.5	2.3	7
Humber Enterprise	1967	200.1	295.4	450	55.4	5.6	2.4	9
Humber Fueller	1957	115.1	192.2	300	42.2	5.5	2.4	8
Humber Mariner	1963	108.5	187	300	42.2	5.3	2.4	8
Humber Navigator	1968	171.2	230	420	45.2	5.9	2.4	8
Humber Pride	1979	225.9	380.8	650	60.8	6	2.4	9
Humber Princess	1979	225.9	380.8	650	60.8	6	2.4	9
Humber Progress	1980	225.9	380.8	650	60.8	6	2.4	9
Humber Renown	1967	200.1	295.4	500	55.4	5.6	2.4	9
Humber Star	1977	144.8	274.6	400	45.7	6.6	2.2	7
Jondor	1950	95	140.8	250	35.4	5.3	2.4	8
Newdale H	1959	121.4	223.1	350	38.1	6.4	2.9	7
Marchdale H	1963	82.2	159.7	275	43.6	5.9	2.4	7
Rebus Stone	1963	101	164.9	275	41.7	5.3	2.4	7
Rufus Stone	1963	101	164.9	275	41.7	5.3	2.4	7
Seagull	1959	107.4	180.4	240	46	5.4	2.3	8

Whitfleet Ltd (1) Humber Area

Farndale H	1967	199.6	293.2	500	55.4	5.6	2.4	9
Fleet Endeavour	1981	234.6	380.3	650	60.8	6	2.4	9
Fleet Enterprise	1983	230.1	380.3	650	60.8	6	2.4	9

John Harker Ltd — Mersey Area

Clyde Enterprise	1960	176.3	262.9	520	45.4	6.3	3	8
Deepdale H	1965	199.9	384.8	600	46.2	8.4	3.4	7
Dovedale H	1962	165.5	305.8	550	47.8	6.6	3.1	7
Humber Jubilee	1977	250.3	382.1	650	60.8	6	2.5	9
Humber Transporter	1967*	310.8	645.5	960	58.9	10.4	2.9	9
Silverdale H	1964	143	300.2	475	43	6.6	3	8
Wharfdale H	1960	390.3	609.1	900	61.8	8.8	2.7	8
Wheatcroft	1957	114.3	188.8	315	42.9	5.3	2.4	8

John Harker Ltd — Tyne/Tees Area

Grovedale H*	1967	170.9	364.6	570	50.3	6.6	3	9
Teesdale H*	1976	301	499	1,050	43.9	9.5	3.9	8

John H. Whitaker — Clyde Area

Borrowdale H	1972	170.3	356.9	550	46.2	6.3	3	8

John H. Whitaker (Holdings) Ltd — Falmouth Area

Ulster Industry (2)	1961	171.1	257.4	500	46.2	6.3	3	8

Top:
John H. Whitaker *Wharfdale H.* *Courtesy: John H. Whitaker*

Above:
Charles M. Willie *Celtic Mariner.* *Courtesy: Fotoflite*

Below:
Wimpey Marine *Wimpey Seahorse.* *Courtesy: Fotoflite*

Although most of the vessels listed above are restricted to estuarial and inland navigations, some, marked (*), have certificates for coastal trading also.

The following are true coastal short-sea traders:

Betty Jean (3+)	1986	552	794	1,360	58.3	9.4	3.9	9
Hoo Venture (4+)	1982	387.7	498.9	1,180	49.9	9.4	4.1	9
Whitank (5)	1975	321.4	682.1	1,011	61.4	9.6	3.7	8
Whitonia (+)	1984	387.7	498.9	1,180	49.9	9.4	4.1	9

Notes: (1) Whitfleet Ltd — a joint venture with Bayford & Co Ltd, and Cawoods Fuels Ltd; (2) water tanker; (3) 50% owned with Bayford & Co Ltd, Leeds; (4) 50% owned with R. Lapthorn & Co Ltd; (+) managed by R. Lapthorn & Co Ltd (qv); (5) Tanker, the other three in this last section being dry cargo vessels.

CHARLES M. WILLIE & CO (SHIPPING) LTD

Celtic House, Roath Basin, Cardiff CF1 5TJ
Tel: (0222) 471000   *Telex:* 498239

Operating what are believed to be the only Cardiff-registered deep-sea cargo ships, Willie started in business as coal merchants in 1913. Ship owning began in 1929. A substantial trade was developed in carrying coal to Biscay ports, returning with pit-props. During the 1960s timber from Portugal became important, and in about 1972 a regular liner service was inaugurated between Watchet and Portugal, followed by others from Mostyn, Shoreham and other UK ports. The line still operates, with chartered ships as well as owned tonnage.

Name	Year	NRT	GRT	DWT	LOA	BM	DFT	SPD
Celtic Ambassador (1)	1977	1,056	1,597	4,554	90.5	14.3	6.4	10.5
Celtic Challenger (2)	1978	1,127	1,555	3,055	80	13.8	5.3	11
Celtic Mariner (2)	1975	586	924	1,519	65.7	10.8	4.2	10.5
Celtic Voyager (2)	1975	586	924	1,519	65.7	10.8	4.2	10.5

Notes: (1) Geared; (2) gearless.

WIMPEY MARINE LTD

Suffolk Road, Great Yarmouth, Norfolk NR31 0ER
Tel: (0493) 656060   *Telex:* 97471/97567

Founded in 1964, this company was ready for the North Sea oil boom and developed a fleet of supply and support vessels which are capable of handling all requirements.

Name	Year	GRT	DWT	LOA	BM	DFT	SPD	BP
Wimpey Seafox (1)	1975	1,380	1,400	64	13.4	5.5	14	100
Wimpey Seahorse (2)	1981	1,599	2,085	69.3	16.1	6.3	15	147
Wimpey Seahunter (2)	1982	1,599	2,085	69.3	16.1	6.3	15	142
Wimpey Seasprite (3)	1986	1,001	1,442	58.9	12.8	4	12	Nil
Wimpey Seatiger (1)	1975	1,380	1,400	64	12.5	5.5	14	100
Wimpey Seawitch (3)	1986	1,001	1,442	58.9	12.8	4	12	Nil

Notes: (1) Anchor handling/supply vessel/tug combined; (2) as (1) plus fire-fighting equipment; (3) supply vessel only.
Several pontoons are also owned by this company.

INDEX TO COMPANIES
(operational 1988)

Front cover:
Furness Withy *Andes*. *FotoFlite, Ashford, Kent*

Back cover:
Sealink *Earl Granville*. *Ambrose Greenway*

Below:
Shell UK *Shell Explorer*. *Courtesy: Fotoflite*